Super Review®

All You Need to Know!

MACROECONOMICS

Robert S. Rycroft, Ph.D.
Chair, Economics Department
Mary Washington College
Fredericksburg, VA

and the Staff of
Research & Education Association
Dr. M. Fogiel, Director

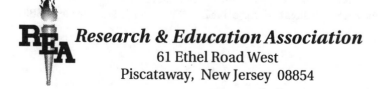

Research & Education Association
61 Ethel Road West
Piscataway, New Jersey 08854

SUPER REVIEW®
OF MACROECONOMICS

Year 2003 Printing

Copyright © 2000 by Research & Education Association. All rights reserved. No part of this book may be reproduced in any form without permission of the publisher.

Printed in the United States of America

Library of Congress Control Number 00-132718

International Standard Book Number 0-87891-189-8

REA's Books Are The Best...
They have rescued lots of grades and more!

(a sample of the <u>hundreds of letters</u> REA receives each year)

"Your books are great! They are very helpful, and have upped my grade in every class. Thank you for such a great product."

Student, Seattle, WA

"Your book has really helped me sharpen my skills and improve my weak areas. Definitely will buy more."

Student, Buffalo, NY

"Compared to the other books that my fellow students had, your book was the most useful in helping me get a great score."

Student, North Hollywood, CA

"I really appreciate the help from your excellent book. Please keep up your great work."

Student, Albuquerque, NM

"Your book was such a better value and was so much more complete than anything your competition has produced (and I have them all)!"

Teacher, Virginia Beach, VA

(more on next page)

(continued from previous page)

" Your books have saved my GPA, and quite possibly my sanity. My course grade is now an 'A', and I couldn't be happier. "

Student, Winchester, IN

" These books are the best review books on the market. They are fantastic! "

Student, New Orleans, LA

" Your book was responsible for my success on the exam. . . I will look for REA the next time I need help. "

Student, Chesterfield, MO

" I think it is the greatest study guide I have ever used! "

Student, Anchorage, AK

" I encourage others to buy REA because of their superiority. Please continue to produce the best quality books on the market. "

Student, San Jose, CA

" Just a short note to say thanks for the great support your book gave me in helping me pass the test . . . I'm on my way to a B.S. degree because of you ! "

Student, Orlando, FL

WHAT THIS Super Review WILL DO FOR YOU

This **Super Review** provides all that you need to know to do your homework effectively and succeed on exams and quizzes.

The book focuses on the core aspects of the subject, and helps you to grasp the important elements quickly and easily.

Outstanding **Super Review** features:

- Topics are covered in logical sequence

- Topics are reviewed in a concise and comprehensive manner

- The material is presented in student-friendly language that makes it easy to follow and understand

- Individual topics can be easily located

- Provides excellent preparation for midterms, finals and in-between quizzes

- In every chapter, reviews of individual topics are accompanied by Questions **Q** and Answers **A** that show how to work out specific problems

- At the end of most chapters, quizzes with answers are included to enable you to practice and test yourself to pinpoint your strengths and weaknesses

- Written by professionals and test experts who function as your very own tutors

Dr. Max Fogiel
Program Director

CONTENTS

CHAPTER 1

Introduction to Economics

1.1 What is Economics?

Economics—"Economics is what economists do." This statement, attributed to the famous economist Jacob Viner, may in fact be the best description of the discipline available. What it says is that economics cannot be defined by a series of topics that all economists study. For example, contrary to widespread belief, economics is **not** the study of business. Topics in business certainly occupy the time of many economists, but there is much more to it. It is more accurate to say that economics is a particular way of looking at topics. **It is a methodology for analyzing situations where human beings have to make choices from limited options**. Consequently, it can be used to study such business-related issues as capital investment, pricing policy, and interest rates, but it can also be used to look at the "bigger" issues of inflation, unemployment, economic growth, and the "non-economic" issues of love, marriage, childbearing, and discrimination, to name but a few.

Macroeconomics—Macroeconomics is the study of the economy as a whole. Some of the topics considered include inflation, unemployment, and economic growth.

Microeconomics—Microeconomics is the study of the individual parts that make up the economy. The parts include households, business firms, and government agencies, and particular emphasis is placed on how these units make decisions and the consequences of these decisions.

1.2 Economic Analysis

Economic Theory—An economic theory is an explanation of why certain economic phenomena occur. For example, there are theories explaining the rate of inflation, how many hours people choose to work, and the amount of goods and services the U.S. will import. Stripped down to essentials, a theory is a set of statements about cause-and-effect relationships in the economy.

Models—A model is an abstract replica of reality and is the formal statement of a theory. The best models retain the essence of the reality, but do away with extraneous details. Virtually all economic analysis is done by first constructing a model of the situation the economist wants to analyze. The reason for this is because human beings are incapable of fully understanding reality. It is too complex for the human mind. Models, because they avoid many of the messier details of reality, can be comprehended, but good models are always "unrealistic."

It would not be inaccurate to say that economists do not analyze the economy, they analyze models of the economy. Almost every prediction that an economist makes, e.g., the impact of changes in the money supply on interest rates, the effect of the unemployment rate on the rate of inflation, the effect of increased competition in an industry on profits, is based on a model.

Models come in verbal, graphical, or mathematical form.

Empirical Analysis—All models yield predictions about the economy. For example, a widely held model predicts that increases in the rate of growth of the money supply will lead to higher inflation. In empirical analysis, economists compare predictions with the actual performance of the economy as measured by economic data. Good empirical analysis often requires mastery of sophisticated statistical and mathematical tools.

Positive Economics —Positive economics is the analysis of "what is." For example, positive economics tries to answer such questions as these: What will the effect be on the rate of inflation if the rate of growth of the money supply is raised by one percentage point? What will happen to hours of work of welfare recipients if welfare benefits are raised $500? What will the effect be on our trade balance if the exchange rate is devalued 5%? Many economists view positive economics as "objective" or "scientific," and believe their special training gives them the expertise to draw conclusions about these types of issues.

Normative Economics—Normative economics is the analysis of "what should be." For example, normative economics tries to answer such questions as these: What inflation rate should our economy strive for? Should welfare recipients be expected to work? Is reducing our trade deficit a desirable thing? Normative economics is clearly a subjective area. There is nothing in an economist's training that gives his or her opinions on these issues any more validity than anyone else's.

Problem Solving Example:

Q Economists construct models for use as tools in interpreting and predicting economic behavior. What are some of the dangers in the use of models?

A The primary danger in constructing an economic model lies in the process of distilling the facts. The economist may eliminate too many facts as irrelevant, severely limiting the validity of the model. For example, if in studying supply and demand of broccoli during a "good year," the economist may neglect to take the weather into account. Hence, the model will work as long as the weather is "good." It will be invalid in a drought year.

The danger in applying models is that it becomes very easy to forget that they are simply generalizations or approximations and people rely too heavily on them. In the above example, 20 years of good weather might lull economists into forgetting that they have left the weather factor out of account so that when drought occurs, they will be unable to account for changes in the broccoli market.

The economist must also keep in mind that economic models have no moral or ethical qualities. They state simply what is, not what ought to be.

1.3 The Economic Way of Thinking

Economics analysis is characterized by an emphasis on certain fundamental concepts.

Scarcity—Human wants and needs (for goods, services, leisure, etc.) exceed the ability of the economy to satisfy those wants and needs. This is true for the economy as a whole as well as each individual in the economy. In other words, there is never enough to go around. Individuals never have enough money to buy all they want. Business firms cannot pay completely satisfactory wages without cutting into profits, and vice versa. Government never has enough money to fund all worthwhile projects. The concept of scarcity is discussed again in Section 2.1.

Opportunity Cost—The reality of scarcity implies that individuals, businesses, and governments must make choices, selecting some opportunities while foregoing others. Buying a car may mean foregoing a vacation; acquiring a new copy machine may mean cancelling the company picnic; paying higher welfare benefits may require terminating a weapons system. The opportunity cost of a choice is the value of the best alternative choice sacrificed.

Individualism—Economic analysis emphasizes individual action. Most economic theories attempt to model the behavior of "typical" individuals. All groups, such as "society," business firms, or unions, are analyzed as a collection of individuals each acting in a particular way. In a sense, the preceding sentence represents an ideal. Not all economic theory achieves this goal.

Rational Behavior—Individuals are assumed to act rationally. This is the most misunderstood term in economics. It does not necessarily mean people are cold, calculating, and greedy. Rather, it means that given a person's goals and knowledge, people take actions likely to achieve those goals and avoid actions likely to detract from those goals. A greedy person acts rationally if he/she spends on himself/herself and does not give to charity. He/she is irrational if he/she does the opposite. An altruistic person acts rationally if he/she gives her money to the needy and does not spend on himself/herself. Irrational behavior is the opposite.

Marginal Analysis—Economists assume that people make choices by weighing the costs and benefits of particular actions.

Problem Solving Example:

 What is "economic rationality"?

Economic rationality refers to a basic assumption made by economists—that human beings are motivated by self-interest and will therefore seek, as their primary goal, the maximization of their own economic position, be it in terms of income, quantity of goods, power and prestige, etc. Economists assume that this is the sole motive of all actors in an economy and that such motives as patriotism, love, etc. will not enter into their economic decision-making processes.

1.4 Other Important Economic Concepts and Terms

Specialization and Division of Labor—This is a strategy for producing goods and services. Division of labor means that different members of a team of producers are given responsibility for different aspects of a production plan. Specialization means that producers become quite apt at those aspects of production they concentrate on. Specialization and division of labor is alleged to lead to efficiency which facilitates economic growth and development.

Problem Solving Example:

 How does specialization, or the "division of labor," increase productivity?

A In a society composed of economically self-sufficient households, each household must produce every variety of good and service which it wishes to consume. Its consumption is limited to what it can produce with its own land, labor, and tools. In a society of specialists, however, each individual or household produces only a very few types of goods or services, which comprise only a small fraction of the types which it may consume. Those types it does not produce directly for itself, it obtains indirectly through exchange with other specialists.

Specialization increases the productivity of a society above that of an otherwise comparable society of self-sufficient households for several reasons. First, it utilizes differences in innate human abilities. Total production of a society is maximized when each task is performed by those whose innate abilities make them the most capable of performing it.

Second, where no differences in innate human abilities exist, specialization over a period of time results in a higher acquired level of skill in one's occupation than one could have achieved without specializing. A society of specialists achieves a higher level of proficiency in productive skills than a society of generalists.

Third, geographic specialization utilizes differences in climate and soil and natural resources. The English climate and soil is ill-suited for growing wine grapes which grow better in Portugal, but better suited for raising sheep. If England specializes in wool textiles and Portugal in wine, their total production of both goods will be greater than if each country produces as much as it can of both goods.

Fourth, specialization saves the time that is lost in production for self-sufficiency in changing tasks. Finally, specialization opens the possibility of discovering and utilizing more technologically advanced techniques, techniques of mass production taking advantage of potential economies of scale.

CHAPTER 2

The Economic Problem

2.1 Universality of the Problem of Scarcity

Goods and Services—Goods and Services refers to anything that satisfies human needs, wants, or desires. Goods are tangible items, such as food, cars, and clothing. Services are intangible items such as education, health care, and leisure. The consumption of goods and services is a source of happiness, well-being, satisfaction, or utility.

Resources (Factors of Production)—Resources refers to anything that can be used to produce goods and services. A commonly-used classification scheme places all resources into one of five categories:

1. *Land*—All natural resources, whether on the land, under the land, in the water, or in the air; e.g., fertile agricultural land, iron ore deposits, tuna fish, corn seeds, and quail.

2. *Labor*—The work effort of human beings.

3. *Capital*—Productive implements made by human beings; e.g., factories, machinery, and tools.

4. *Entrepreneurship*—A specialized form of labor. Entrepreneurship is creative labor. It refers to the ability to detect new business opportunities and bring them to fruition. Entrepreneurs also manage the other factors of production.

5. *Technology*—The practical application of scientific knowledge. Technology is typically combined with the other factors to make them more productive.

Scarcity—Economists assume that human wants and needs are virtually limitless while acknowledging that the resources to satisfy those needs are limited. Consequently, society is never able to produce enough goods and services to satisfy everybody, or most anyone, completely. Alternatively, resources are scarce relative to human needs and desires.

Scarcity is a problem of all societies, whether rich or poor. As a mental experiment, write down the amount of income you think a typical family needs to be "comfortable" in the United States today: _____. Now compare your figure with the median family income in the United States found on page 53. In most instances, what students think is necessary to be comfortable far exceeds median family income, which loosely implies that the typical family in the U.S. is not comfortable, even though we are the richest nation in the history of the world. If your figure is less than median income, think again. Do you think you would really be "comfortable" at that level of income?

Problem Solving Example:

Define "scarcity" in economic terms. From what does economic scarcity result?

Goods or resources are considered "scarce," in economic terms, if they are not available in sufficient quantity to satisfy all wants for them. Scarcity therefore results from a combination of two factors: quantities of goods are limited and desire for goods is unlimited. Since wants for virtually all goods are greater than the available supply, most resources are scarce. Only "free goods," such as air (in most situations), are not scarce.

2.2 Universal Problems Caused by Scarcity

A society without scarcity is a society without problems, and, consequently, one where there is no need to make decisions. In the real world, all societies must make three crucial decisions:

1. **What goods and services to produce and in what quantities.**

2. **How to produce the goods and services selected**—what resource combinations and production techniques to use.

3. **How to distribute the goods and services produced among people**—who gets how much of each good and service produced.

Problem Solving Example:

 What are the three fundamental problems of any society?

 "What, how, and for whom" are the three basic problems of any economic society.

The problem of "what" is: what commodities shall be produced and in what quantities. Do we want, for example, more to eat and less clothing, or vice versa.

The question of "how" asks how shall goods be produced. Who shall do the producing, with what resources, and in what technological manner?

Finally we ask, "For whom shall goods be produced?" How shall we distribute what we produce? Shall all goods be distributed equally among all individuals? Or by what principle shall distribution of goods be distributed among individuals? According to their need, according to their contribution to production, or by some other rule?

2.3 Universal Economic Goals

Allocative (Economic) Efficiency—A society achieves allocative efficiency if it produces the types and quantities of goods and services that most satisfies its people. Failure to do so wastes resources.

Technical Efficiency—A society achieves technical efficiency when it is producing the greatest quantity of goods and services possible from its resources. Failure to do so is also a waste of resources.

Equity—A society wants the distribution of goods and services to conform with its notions of "fairness."

Standards of Equity—Equity is not necessarily synonymous with equality. There is no objective standard of equity, and all societies have different notions of what constitutes equity. Three widely held standards are:

1. **Contributory standard**—Under a contributory standard, people are entitled to a share of goods and services based on what they contribute to society. Those making larger contributions receive correspondingly larger shares. The measurement of contribution and what to do about those who contribute very little or are unable to contribute (i.e., the disabled) are continuing issues.

2. **Needs standard**—Under a needs standard, a person's contribution to society is irrelevant. Goods and services are distributed based on the needs of different households. Measuring need and inducing people to contribute to society when goods and services are guaranteed are continuing issues.

3. **Equality Standard**—Under an equality standard, every person is entitled to an equal share of goods and services, simply because they are a human being. Allowing for needs and inducing people to make maximum productive efforts when reward is the same for all, are continuing issues.

Economists remain divided over whether the goals of equity and efficiency (allocative and technical) are complementary or in conflict.

Problem Solving Example:

 What are some widely held economic goals of society?

Some of the primary goals of an economic system are economic growth, full employment, price stability, economic freedom and equitable distribution of income, and economic security. (It should be noted, however, that these are by no means universal goals.)

An economic system attempts to ensure, by the production of certain types of goods and services (e.g., capital goods, education), a growing standard of living, i.e., economic growth brought about by the production of more and better goods in the future.

Society attempts to obtain the maximum use, e.g., full employment, of all its factors of production.

In order to facilitate economic activity, severe fluctuations in the price level (inflation or deflation) are to be avoided.

To allow for change, innovation, and eventually efficiency, a great degree of freedom in the determination of each individual's employment of his/her productive resources is sought.

An equitable distribution of income: to some people means that great disparities between society's richest and poorest are unacceptable.

Economic society refers to the attempt to provide for those members of society who are, for one reason or another, unable to produce.

2.4 Production Possibilities Curve

The Production Possibilities Curve is a model of the economy used to illustrate the problems associated with scarcity. It shows the maximum feasible combinations of two goods or services that society can produce, assuming all resources are used in their most productive manner.

ASSUMPTIONS OF THE MODEL

1. Society is only capable of producing two goods (guns and butter).

2. At a given point in time, society has a fixed quantity of resources.

3. All resources are used in their most productive manner.

Table 2.1 shows selected combinations of the two goods that can be produced given the assumptions.

Point	Guns	Butter
A	0	16
B	4	14
C	7	12
D	9	9
E	10	5
F	11	0

Table 2.1 Selected Combinations of Guns and Butter

Figure 2.1 is a graphical depiction of the production possibilities curve (curve FA).

Technical Efficiency–All points on the curve are points of technical efficiency. By definition, technical efficiency is achieved when more of one good cannot be produced without producing less of the other good. Find point D on the curve. Any move to a point with more guns (i.e., point E) will necessitate a reduction in butter production. Any move to a point with more butter (such as point C) will necessitate a reduction in guns production. Any point inside the curve (such as point G) represents technical inefficiency. Either inefficient production methods are being used or resources are not fully employed. A movement from G to the curve will allow more of one or both goods to be produced without any reduction in the quantity of the other good. Points outside the curve (such as H) are technically infeasible given society's current stock of resources and technological knowledge.

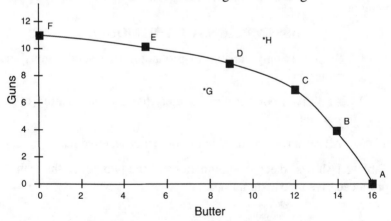

Figure 2.1 Production Possibilities Curve

Opportunity Cost—Consider a move from D to E. Society gets one more unit of guns, but must sacrifice four units of butter. The four units of butter is the opportunity cost of the gun. One gun costs four units of butter.

Law of Increasing Costs—Starting from point A and moving up along the curve, note that the opportunity cost of guns increases. From point A to B, two butter are sacrificed to get four guns (one gun costs one-half butter); from point B to C, two butter are sacrificed to get three guns (one gun costs two-thirds butter); from C to D, three butter are sacrificed for two guns (one gun costs one and one-half butter); from D to E, one gun costs four butter; from E to F, one gun costs five butter.

The law of increasing costs says that as more of a good or service is produced, its opportunity cost will rise. It is a consequence of resources being specialized in particular uses. Some resources are particularly good in gun production and not so good for butter production, and vice versa.

At the commencement of gun production, the resources shifted out of butter will be those least productive in butter (and most productive in guns). Consequently, gun production will rise with little cost in terms of butter. As more resources are diverted, those more productive in butter will be affected, and the opportunity cost will rise. This is what gives the production possibilities curve its characteristic convex shape.

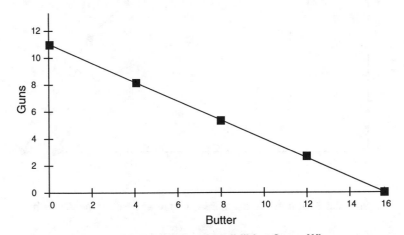

Figure 2.2 Production Possibilities Curve When Resources Not Specialized

If resources are not specialized in particular uses, opportunity costs will remain constant and the production possibilities curve will be a straight line (see Figure 2.2 on previous page).

Allocative Efficiency—Allocative efficiency will be represented by the point on the curve that best satisfies society's needs and wants. It cannot be located without additional knowledge of society's likes and dislikes. A complicating factor is that the allocatively efficient point is not independent of society's distribution of income and wealth.

Economic Growth—Society's production of goods and services is limited by its resources. Economic growth, then, requires that society increases the amount of resources it has or makes those resources more productive through the application of technology. Graphically, economic growth is represented by an outward shift of the curve to IJ (see Table 2.3). Economic growth will make more combinations of goods and services feasible, but it will not end the problem of scarcity.

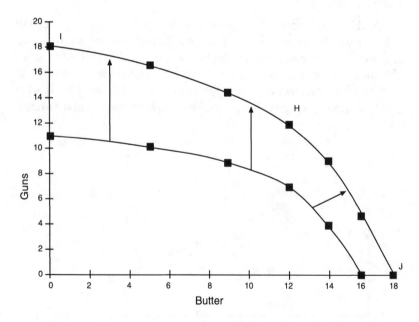

Figure 2.3 Production Possibilities Curve and Economic Growth

CHAPTER 3

Demand and Supply

3.1 Demand

Demand—Demand is a schedule or a graph showing the relationship between the price of a product and the amount consumers are willing and able to buy, ceteris paribus. The schedule or graph does not necessarily show what consumers actually buy at each price. The Law of Demand says there is an inverse relationship between price and quantity demanded, people will be willing and able to buy more if the product gets cheaper.

CETERIS PARIBUS

All hypothetical relationships between variables in economics include a stated or implied assumption ceteris paribus. The term means "all other factors held constant." As we will see, there are many factors affecting the amount of a product people are willing and able to buy. The demand schedule shows the relationship between price and quantity demanded, holding all the other factors constant. This allows us to investigate the independent effect that price changes have on quantity demanded without worrying about the influence the other factors are having.

Demand Schedule—Assume the product is widgets. Let Qd be quantity demanded and P be price.

Qd	P
48.0	1.00
47.5	1.25
47.0	1.50
46.5	1.75
46.0	2.00

Demand Graph—See Figure 3.1.

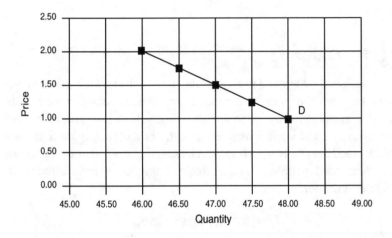

Figure 3.1 Graph of Demand Schedule

Problem Solving Example:

 Define the term "demand" in economics. Give an example to illustrate demand.

Demand is defined as a schedule which shows the various amounts of a product which consumers are willing and able to purchase at each specific price in a set of possible prices during some specified period of time. Note the phrase, "willing and able," because willingness alone is not effective in the market. One may be willing to buy a Mercedes-Benz, but if this willingness is not backed by the ability to buy, that is, by the necessary dollars it will not be effective and, therefore will not be reflected in the market. The table represents hypothetical data for an individual buyer's demand for corn.

Price per bushel	Quantity demanded per week
$5	10
4	20
3	35
2	55
1	80

The demand schedule in and of itself does not indicate which of the five possible prices will actually exist in the corn market. This depends on both demand and supply. Demand is simply a tabular statement of a buyer's plans, or intentions, with respect to the purchase of a product.

It is important to note that to be meaningful, the quantities demanded at each price must relate to some specific time period—a day, a week, a month, and so forth. The phrase "a consumer will buy 10 bushels of corn at $5 per bushel" is vague and meaningless. The phrase "a consumer will buy 10 bushels of corn per week at $5 per bushel," however, is clear and very meaningful.

3.2 Supply

Supply—Supply is a schedule or a graph showing the relationship between the price of a product and the amount producers are willing and able to supply, ceteris paribus. The schedule or graph does not necessarily show what producers actually sell at each price. There is generally a positive relationship between price and quantity supplied, reflecting higher costs associated with greater production.

Supply Schedule—Assume the product is widgets. Let Qs be quantity supplied.

Qs	P
46.0	1.00
46.5	1.25
47.0	1.50
47.5	1.75
48.0	2.00

Supply Graph—See Figure 3.2

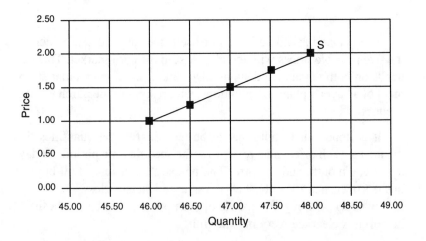

Figure 3.2 Graph of Supply Schedule

Problem Solving Example:

What is meant by the term "supply," and what is a "supply curve"?

The "supply" of a good refers to the relationship, at a particular time, between the price offered for the good and the quantity of it that sellers are willing to sell. The quantity of a good that an individual or group is willing to sell depends, other factors being equal, on the per unit price of the good. Or, to describe the same relationship in a different way, the minimum per unit price which will induce an individual or some members of the group to sell units of the good depends on the number of units, other factors again being equal.

A supply curve is a graphic representation of the relationship between the (hypothetical) price of a good and the quantity supplied.

Let the table represent Jones' supply schedule of watermelons on a Fourth of July:

Price	$1	$2	$3	$3.50	$4	$4.50	$5	$5.50	$6	$7	$8	$9
Quantity	0	0	1	2	3	4	5	6	7	8	9	10

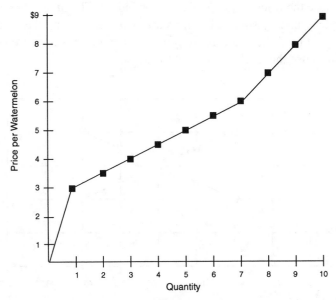

The information in the table can be presented in graphic form as Jones' supply curve, as shown in the figure.

3.3 Market Equilibrium

The intersection of the demand and supply curves indicates the equilibrium price and quantity in the market (see Figure 3.3). The word equilibrium is synonymous with stable. The price and quantity in a market will frequently not be equal to the equilibrium, but if that is the case then the market will be adjusting, and, hence, not stable.

If the price of the product is $2.00, then the quantity supplied of the product (48) will be greater than the quantity demanded (46). There will be a surplus in the market of 48 – 46 = 2. The unsold product will force producers to lower their prices. A reduction in price will reduce the quantity supplied while increasing quantity demanded until the surplus disappears. Two dollars is not an equilibrium because the market is forced to adjust.

If the price of the product is $1.00, then the quantity supplied of the product (46) will be less than the quantity demanded (48). There will be a shortage in the market of 48 – 46 = 2. Unsatisfied customers will cause the price of the product to be bid up. The higher price will cause the quantity supplied to increase while decreasing the quantity demanded until the shortage disappears. One dollar is not an equilibrium because the market is forced to adjust.

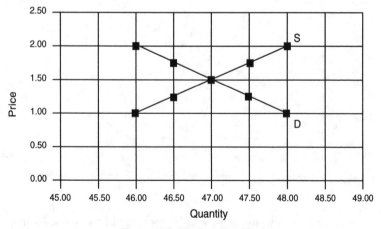

Figure 3.3 Market Equilibrium

If the price of the product is $1.50, then the quantity demanded (47) is just equal to the quantity supplied (47). Producers can sell all they want. Buyers can buy all they want. Since everyone is satisfied, there is no reason for the price to change. Hence, $1.50 is an equilibrium price and 47 is an equilibrium quantity.

3.4   Shifts in Demand

Price is not the only factor affecting the amount consumers are willing and able to buy. Other factors include:

1. Consumer tastes,

2. Income,

3. Prices of other goods, and

4. Price expectations.

Graphically, the effect of these factors can be represented by shifts in the demand curve (see Figure 3.4). A rightward/outward/upward shift in the curve is an increase in demand (*D* to *D′*). Events that increase the willingness and ability of consumers to buy will increase demand. Alternatively, events that would increase the price consumers would be willing to pay for the product will increase demand. A leftward/inward/downward shift in the curve is a decrease in demand (*D* to *D″*). Events that decrease the willingness and ability of consumers to buy will decrease demand. Alternatively, events that would decrease the price that consumers would pay for a good would decrease demand.

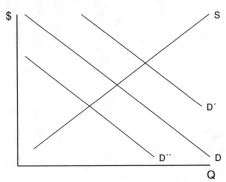

Figure 3.4 Shifts in the Demand Curve

Factor	Event	Shift Demand Curve	Equilibrium Price	Equilibrium Quantity
Tastes	Consumers prefer product more	out	increase	increase
	Consumers prefer product less	in	decrease	decrease
Income	Normal good — income increases	out	increase	increase
	Normal good — income decreases	in	decrease	decrease
	Inferior good — income increases	in	decrease	decrease
	Inferior good — income decreases	out	increase	increase
Price of Related Goods	Substitute good — price increases	out	increase	increase
	Substitute good — price decreases	in	decrease	decrease
	Complement good — price increases	in	decrease	decrease
	Complement good — price decreases	out	increase	increase
Price Expectations	Price level expected to rise	out	increase	increase
	Price level expected to fall	in	decrease	decrease

Table 3.1 Shifts in the Demand Curve

Normal Good or Service—A good or service that consumers want to buy more of when their income rises, e.g., filet mignon.

Inferior Good or Service—A good or service that consumers want to buy less of when their income rises, e.g., a generic brand of aspirin.

Substitute Good or Service—A good or service that can be used in place of another good or service, e.g., wheat bread and white bread.

Complement Good or Service—A good or service whose use increases the enjoyment a consumer gets from another good or service, e.g., bread and butter, butter makes bread taste better.

Change in Demand v. Change in Quantity Demanded—Factors that shift the demand curve cause changes in demand. These are changes in income, tastes, prices of other goods, and price expectations. Note that changes in the price of the product is not included on this list. A movement from one point to another along an existing demand curve represents a change in quantity demanded. This can only result from a change in the price of the product.

Problem Solving Example:

What are some of the major determinants of the demand for a good?

Some of the major determinants of the demand for a good are:

1. Tastes of consumers,

2. The number of potential buyers and their incomes,

3. The prices of substitute and complementary goods, and

4. Consumer expectations of future prices and their future incomes.

Demand has been defined as desire plus ability to buy. Consumer tastes determine their desires to buy various goods. The greater their taste for a good, the more they will buy at a given price, or the higher the price they are willing to pay for a given quantity.

Similarly, with given tastes for a good, the quantity that consumers demand at a given price is generally greater, the greater their incomes.

The prices of other goods in the market also affect the demand for any good. Relatively low prices for goods which are regarded as close substitutes for the goods under consideration (e.g., margarine for butter) mean less demand for that good, whereas relatively high prices for substitutes mean more demand for it. Prices of complementary goods, i.e., goods that are often consumed in conjunction with the good in question (e.g., bread and butter) have a different effect. A relatively high price for complementary goods means less demand for the good in question, while relatively low prices mean a greater demand for it.

Finally consumers' expectations of their future incomes and of future prices affect their current demands for goods. If consumers expect to have greater incomes in the future than they have presently, they will tend to demand greater quantities of at least some goods than if they expected their incomes to remain the same. And, of course, they will demand less if they expect their incomes to fall. Also, expectations of a higher price in the future will stimulate a greater present demand for a good than there would be if its price were expected to remain at its current height. And, naturally, expectations of a lower price in the future will cause buyers to delay some of their purchases and thus reduce current demand.

3.5 Shifts in Supply

Price is not the only factor affecting the amount producers are willing and able to supply. Other factors include:

1. Costs of resources,

2. Changes in technology,

3. Unexpected events,

4. Price expectations, and

5. Direct taxes on the product.

Graphically, the effect of these factors can be represented by shifts in the supply curve (see Figure 3.5). A rightward/outward/downward shift in the curve is an increase in supply (*S* to *S´*). Events that would increase the willingness and ability of firms to supply output would increase supply. Alternatively, events that would lower the cost of producing any level of output would increase supply. A leftward/inward/upward shift in the curve is a decrease in supply (*S* to *S´´*). Events that would decrease the willingness and ability of firms to supply output would decrease supply. Alternatively, events that would raise the cost of producing output would decrease supply.

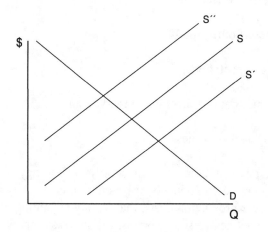

Figure 3.5 Shifts in the Supply Curve

Change in Supply v. Change in Quantity Supplied—Factors that shift the supply curve cause changes in supply. These are changes in cost of resources, technology, unexpected events, price expectations, and direct taxes. Note that the price of the product is not included on this list. A movement from one point to another along an existing supply curve represents a change in supply. This can only result from a change in the price of the product.

Problem Solving Example:

List the basic nonprice determinants of supply. Explain how each affects the supply curve.

The basic nonprice determinants of supply are:

1. The technique of production (technology),

2. Resource prices,

3. Prices of other goods,

4. Price expectations,

5. The number of sellers in the market, and

6. Taxes and subsidies.

The first two determinants of supply, technology and resource prices, are the two components of production costs. Anything which serves to lower production costs, that is, any technological improvement or any decline in resource prices, will increase supply. With lower costs, businesses will find it profitable to offer a larger amount of the product at each possible price. An increase in the price of resources (a deterioration of technology being unlikely) will cause a decrease in supply.

Changes in the prices of other goods can also shift the supply curve for a product. A decline in the price of wheat may cause a farmer to produce and offer more corn at each possible price. Conversely, a rise in the price of wheat may make farmers less willing to produce and offer corn in the market.

Expectations concerning the future price of a product can also affect a producer's current willingness to supply that product. Farmers might withhold some of their current corn harvest from the market, anticipating a higher corn price in the future. This will cause a decrease in the current supply of corn. On the other hand, in many types of manufacturing, expected price increases may induce firms to expand production immediately, causing supply to increase.

Given the scale of operations of each firm, the larger the number of suppliers, the greater will be market supply. The smaller the number of firms in an industry, the less the market supply will be.

Finally, certain taxes, such as sales taxes, add to production costs and therefore reduce supply. Conversely, subsidies lower costs and increase supply.

A change in one or more of the determinants of supply will cause a change in supply. An increase in supply shifts the supply curve to the right. A decrease in supply is shown graphically as a movement of the curve to the left. A change in the quantity supplied involves a movement, caused by a change in the price of the product under consideration, from one point to another on a fixed supply curve.

3.6 Price Controls

An equilibrium price is not necessarily a "fair" price. It could happen that the equilibrium price in a market is higher than society considers "fair." It could also happen that an equilibrium price in a market is lower than society considers "fair." There has been a long history of governments imposing price controls in markets where prices are considered a "problem."

Price Ceiling—A price ceiling is a government mandated level above which a price cannot go. Price ceilings are frequently set where equilibrium prices promise to be "too high." An example would be rent controls in cities. An often unappreciated side-effect of a price ceiling is to create an artificial shortage of the product and to lead to black markets in the product.

Factor	Event	Shift Supply Curve	Equilibrium Price	Equilibrium Quantity
Costs of Resources	Resource costs increase	in	increase	decrease
	Resource costs decrease	out	decrease	increase
Technology	Technology advances	out	decrease	increase
	Technology retreats	in	increase	decrease
Unexpected Events	Product destruction	in	increase	decrease
Price Expectations	Product price expected to rise	in	increase	decrease
	Product price expected to fall	out	decrease	increase
Taxes	direct taxes on product rise	in	increase→	decrease→
	direct taxes on product fall	out	decrease→	increase→

Table 3.2 Shifts in the Supply Curve

In the market (see Figure 3.6) the equilibrium price is $1.50 and equilibrium quantity is 47. If government imposes a price ceiling preventing prices from rising above $1.00, producers will reduce quantity supplied to 46 while consumers will increase their quantity demanded to 48. A shortage of 48 – 46 = 2 will result.

Price Floor—A price floor is a government mandated level below which a price cannot go. Price floors are frequently set where equilibrium prices promise to be "too low." An example would be the minimum wage. An often unappreciated side-effect of a price floor is to create an artificial surplus (e.g., unemployment) of the item and to lead to black markets.

In the market, the equilibrium price is $1.50, and equilibrium quantity is 47. If government imposes a price floor preventing prices from falling below $2.00, producers will increase their quantity supplied to 48 while consumers reduce their quantity demanded to 46. A surplus of 48 – 46 = 2 will result.

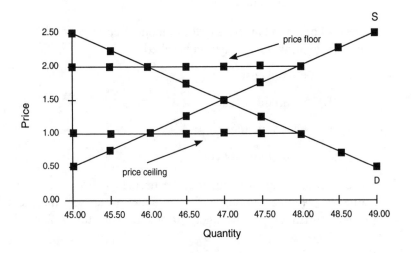

Figure 3.6 Price Controls

Quiz: Introduction to Economics— Demand and Supply

1. Among the various definitions of economics, which of the following is most widely used?

    (A) The study of exchange (with or without money) between people

    (B) The study of how production and consumption activities are organized

    (C) The study of wealth

    (D) The study of how people choose to use scarce or limited productive resources to produce various commodities and distribute them to various members of society for consumption

2. The cost of a good in terms of the amount of other goods forgone in order to allow its production is called

    (A) a fixed cost.

    (B) a variable cost.

    (C) economic rent.

    (D) an opportunity cost.

3. The economizing problem may be defined as the attempt to allocate resources among various production uses in the most efficient manner. The necessity of dealing with the problem is caused by

    (A) the law of increasing costs.

    (B) scarcity.

(C) the "Invisible Hand" doctrine.

(D) the division of labor.

4. The production possibility (or transformation) curve illustrates the basic principle that

(A) an economy will automatically seek that level of output at which all of its resources are employed.

(B) an economy's capacity to produce increases in proportion to its population size.

(C) if all the resources of an economy are in use, more of one good can be produced only if less of another good is produced.

(D) None of the above.

5. The production possibility curve of two goods is usually drawn concave, as viewed from the origin, because

(A) all resources are scarce.

(B) of the Law of Diminishing Returns.

(C) not all economic resources can be used equally efficiently in the alternative uses.

(D) of a convention.

6. Assume that the demand for product A is downward sloping. If the price of A falls from $3.00 to $2.75

(A) the demand for A will fall.

(B) the demand for A will rise.

(C) the quantity demanded of A will fall.

(D) the quantity demanded of A will rise.

7. One reason why the quantity demanded of a good tends to rise as its price falls is that

    (A) the decrease in price shifts the supply downward.

    (B) the decrease in price shifts the demand curve upward.

    (C) people's real incomes are greater so they increase their consumption of the good.

    (D) demand has to rise to restore equilibrium after a price fall.

8. As the equilibrium price of butter decreases

    (A) the demand curve for margarine shifts to the left and downward.

    (B) the demand curve for margarine shifts to the right and upward.

    (C) the demand curve for margarine remains the same.

    (D) the supply curve for margarine shifts left and downward.

9. If the demand curve for product B shifts to the right as the price of product A declines, it can be concluded that

    (A) A and B are substitutes.

    (B) A and B are complementary goods.

    (C) A is an inferior good and B is a superior good.

    (D) A is a superior good and B is an inferior good.

10. Price ceilings and price floors

    (A) shift supply and demand curves and, therefore, have no effect on the rationing of prices.

    (B) clear the market.

    (C) always result in shortages.

    (D) interfere with the rationing function of prices.

ANSWER KEY

1.	(D)	6.	(D)
2.	(D)	7.	(C)
3.	(B)	8.	(A)
4.	(C)	9.	(B)
5.	(C)	10.	(D)

CHAPTER 4

Economic Systems

4.1 Types of Systems

Every society must have some method for making the basic economic decisions defined in 2.2.

Tradition—Traditional systems largely rely on custom to determine production and distribution questions. While not static, traditional systems are slow to change and are not well-equipped to propel a society into sustained growth. Traditional systems are found in many of the poorer Third World countries.

Command—Command economies rely on a central authority to make decisions. The central authority may be a dictator or a democratically constituted government.

Market—It is easier to describe what a market system is not than what it is. In a pure market system, there is no central authority and custom plays very little role. Every consumer makes buying decisions based on his or her own needs and desires and income. Individual self-interest rules. Every producer decides for him- or herself what goods or services to produce, what price to charge, what resources to employ, and what production methods to use. Producers are motivated solely by profit considerations. There is vigorous competition in every market.

Mixed—A mixed economy contains elements of each of the three systems defined on the previous page. All real world economies are mixed economies, although the mixture of tradition, command, and market differs greatly. The U.S. economy has traditionally placed great emphasis on the market, although there is a large and active government (command) sector. The Soviet economy places main reliance on government to direct economic activity, but there is a small market sector.

Capitalism—The key characteristic of a capitalistic economy is that productive resources are owned by private individuals.

Socialism—The key characteristic of a socialist economy is that productive resources are owned collectively by society. Alternatively, productive resources are under the control of government.

Problem Solving Examples:

Q What is a "mixed economy"?

 A "mixed economy" is one in which some of the means of production are privately owned and some are owned and operated by government. It is also characterized by government policies which attempt the following: 1) avoid general business fluctuations, 2) alter the distribution of wealth from the free market pattern in such a way as to provide every individual with at least a certain minimum income, 3) regulate working conditions in private industry, 4) regulate business behavior (mergers, product safety, etc.) in the market. It is thus a system resulting from the modification of the pure type of free market capitalism by interventions characteristic of socialist economies.

Virtually all countries today have some variety of a mixed economy. There is none in which either the pure capitalist type or the pure socialist, centrally-planned type exists unmodified.

What are the essential features of a socialist economy?

A socialist economy is a specialized economy (i.e., one employing the principle of the division of labor) in which the means of production are controlled by the state and production operations are centrally planned by an agency of the state (the central planning board or commission). The central planning board sets priorities and physical production targets for all commodities, and determines the physical quantities of all resources, including labor, to be used as inputs in the production of each commodity.

Consumers have no direct voice in production decisions. They may have a choice in what they consume, however, subject to the limits imposed by the central planners' decisions regarding the production of consumers' goods. If consumption goods are not distributed by command, then consumers are free to buy consumption goods in markets at government-set prices. Laborers may be assigned to their jobs or the central planners may set wage rates in such a way as to try to achieve the allocation of labor among industries called for by their plan.

4.2 Circular Flow

The Circular Flow is a model of economic relationships in a capitalistic market economy. Households, the owners of all productive resources, supply resources to firms through the resource markets, receiving monetary payments in return. Firms use the resources purchased (or rented, as the case may be) to produce goods and services, which are then sold to households and other businesses in the product markets. Household income not spent (consumed) may be saved in the financial markets. Firms may borrow from the financial markets to finance capital expansion (investment). Firm saving and household borrowing are not shown.

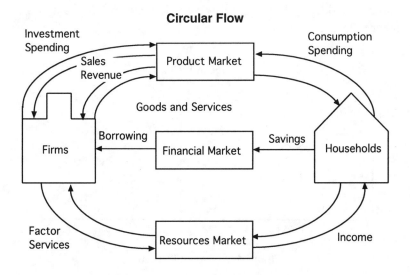

Figure 4.1 The Circular Flow

4.3   How a Market Economy Works

Although the description of a market economy may suggest that chaos is the order of the day, economists believe that if certain conditions are met, a market economy is easily capable of achieving the major economic goals.

How a Market Economy Achieves Allocation Efficiency—Market forces will lead firms to produce the mix of goods most desired. Unforeseen events can be responded to in a rational manner.

4.3.1   Change in Tastes

Assume a change in consumer tastes from beef to chicken (see Figure 4.2). An increase in demand in the chicken market will be accompanied by a decrease in demand in the beef market. The higher price of chicken will attract more resources into the market and lead to an increase in the quantity supplied. The lower price of beef will induce a reduction in the quantity supplied and exit of resources to other industries.

Change in Tastes

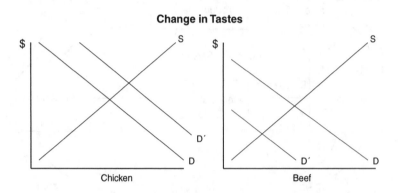

Figure 4.2 Change in Tastes

Note that the change in the level of output of both goods occurred because it was in the economic self-interest of firms to do so. Greater demand in the chicken market increased the profitability of chicken; lower demand in the beef market decreased the profitability of beef. Chicken and beef producers responded to society's desires not out of a sense of public spiritedness, but out of self-interest.

Problem Solving Example:

 Is pure capitalism adaptable to changes in consumer tastes?

A Pure capitalism adapts to a change in consumer tastes in two ways. Production of consumer goods adjusts to changes in tastes, and the resource markets adjust to changes in the production of consumer goods.

In pure capitalism, if consumer tastes change (for example, if consumers want more sandals and fewer shoes), these changes will be reflected in the demands for the two goods. In the market for sandals, consumers will bid against each other for limited quantity of sandals available. In the shoe market, firms will undercut each other in an effort to sell some of the unwanted shoes. The price of sandals will rise, leading to higher profits in the industry. The price of shoes will fall, leading to lower profits in the shoe industry. The higher profits in the sandal industry will induce firms to expand their output of sandals, leading to an increased supply of sandals. The losses in the shoe industry will drive some firms out of the shoe industry, thus reducing the supply of shoes. The effect of the changes in consumer tastes has been reflected in changes in production; more sandals and fewer shoes are being produced.

The analysis so far assumes that resource markets will adjust to these changes. A sandal-making firm earning high profits will be able to pay more for resources—higher wages, for example. By paying higher wages, the firm will attract more workers. Similarly, a firm losing money in the shoe business will be forced to cut wages, prompting workers to leave. Resources, in effect, will shift in response to changes in producers' demands, and indirectly, in response to changes in consumer tastes.

4.3.2 Scarcity

An unexpected freeze in Florida will shift in the supply curve of orange juice, driving up its price, and causing consumers to cut back their purchases (see Figure 4.3). The higher price of orange juice will increase the demand for substitute products like apple juice, causing an increase in the quantity supplied of apple juice to take the place of orange juice.

Freeze in Florida

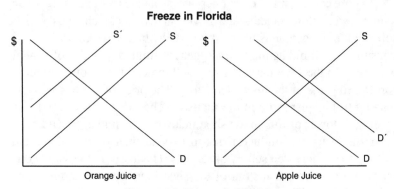

Figure 4.3 Freeze in Florida

As above, the reaction of market participants reflected their evaluation of their own self-interest. Consumers reduced their quantity demanded of orange juice because it was now more expensive. Apple juice producers expanded production because now it was more profitable.

Consumer Sovereignty—"The Consumer is King." Consumer sovereignty means that consumers determine what is produced in the economy. In a market economy, business must cater to the whims of consumer tastes or else go out of business.

How a Market Economy Achieves Technical Efficiency—Market forces will lead firms to produce output in the most efficient manner. The constant struggle for profits will stimulate firms to cut costs. Note that technical efficiency results from attention to self-interest, not the public interest.

The Importance of Competition—A market economy thrives on competition between firms. In their struggle for survival, firms will be forced to cater to consumer demand (leading to allocative efficiency) and force production costs down as far as possible (leading to technical efficiency).

How a Market Economy Achieves Full Employment—Full employment of resources is thought to be the normal state of affairs in a market economy. Resource surpluses will force down the resource's price, leading quickly to re-employment.

How a Market Economy Achieves Growth—Competition between firms for the consumer's dollar will force a constant search for better products and methods of production. The resulting technological change will lead to optimal growth.

The Market Economy and Equity—This is a problematic area for a market economy. Certainly there are financial rewards for those who produce the products that win consumer acceptance. There are losses for those who do not. Yet winners in a market economy are not necessarily the most virtuous of people, they just sell a better product. While consumer demand determines the pattern of production, those consumers with the most income exert the greatest influence on the pattern.

The Role of Prices in a Market Economy—In order for an economy to operate efficiently, there must be information and incentives. There must be information on what goods and services are in demand, which resources are scarce, and so on. There must be an incentive to produce the goods and services desired, conserve on scarce resources, and so on. Both information and incentives are provided by prices.

High prices indicate goods and services in demand; low prices indicate goods and services that have lost favor. High prices indicate scarce resources; low prices indicate plentiful. Firms responding "properly" to high prices will earn profits; firms responding "properly" to low prices will avoid losses. Firms exploiting cheap resources will earn profits; firms conserving on expensive resources will avoid losses.

Assuming the conditions in Section 4.5 are met, prices always provide accurate information and appropriate incentives. Since traditional and command economies downplay the role of prices, they have a much more difficult time achieving allocational and technical efficiency.

4.4   Adam Smith and *The Wealth of Nations*

Adam Smith—Adam Smith (1723–1790) was a Scottish economist whose writing can be said to have inaugurated the modern era of economic analysis.

The Wealth of Nations—Published in 1776, *The Wealth of Nations* can be read as an analysis of a market economy. It was Smith's belief that a market economy was a superior form of organization from the standpoint of both economic progress and human liberty.

Invisible Hand—Smith acknowledged that self-interest was a dominant motivating force in a market economy, yet this self-interest was ultimately consistent with the public interest. Market participants were guided by an invisible hand to act in ways that promoted the public interest. Firms may only be concerned with profits, but profits are only earned by firms that satisfy consumer demand and keep costs down.

Problem Solving Example:

Q   Who was Adam Smith, and what is the principle of the "Invisible Hand"? In what situation will this principle not hold true?

A   Adam Smith was an eighteenth-century Scottish professor of moral philosophy who is generally credited with founding economics as a science. His book, *The Wealth of Nations*, published in 1776, was the first notable attempt to explain the workings of a free market. In his book, Smith sets forth the principle of the "Invisible Hand," which asserts that if each individual in society acts in such a way as to maximize his own gain, the functioning of the free market will assure, as a result, the maximum possible benefit to society as a whole.

The Wealth of Nations is undoubtedly the foundation work of modern economic thought. The principles of the book are simple. First, Smith assumes that the prime psychological drive in man as an economic being is the drive of self-interest. Secondly, he contends that in a free market system, one's self-interest is best served by serving that of others. Since it is in the producer's interest to produce something which will be demanded by the public, it follows that the pursuit of one's own self-interest will automatically serve the interest of society. Finally, from these postulates, he concludes that the best program is for government to leave the economic process completely alone—what has come to be known as laissez-faire, economic liberalism or non-interventionism.

In formulating the principle of the "Invisible Hand," Smith assumed the existence of perfect competition—a market system with no artificial restrictions or elements of monopoly power. Since government restricts the market in order to compensate for externalities such as pollution, firms are restrained in pursuing their self-interest. Also, some firms have a degree of monopoly power, and therefore are not compelled to accept the wishes of society as guides for their own decision making.

4.5 Conditions That Must Be Met For a Market Economy to Achieve Allocative and Technical Efficiency

A market economy will automatically produce the optimum quantity of every good or service at the lowest possible cost if four conditions are met:

Adequate Information—Consumers must be well-enough informed about prices, quality and availability of products, and other matters that they can make intelligent spending decisions. Workers must be well-enough informed about wages and working conditions that they can choose wisely among job opportunities. Other segments of the economy must be similarly well-informed.

Competition—There must be vigorous competition in every market. Monopolistic elements will reduce output, *raise prices*, and allow inefficiency in particular markets.

No Externalities—Externalities exist when a transaction between a buyer and seller affects an innocent third party. An example would be if *A* buys a product from *B* that *B* produced under conditions that polluted the air that others breathe. (Not all externalities result in damage to society. Some are beneficial.) Where externalities are present, there is the possibility of over- or under-production of particular goods and services.

No Public Goods—The market is unlikely to produce the appropriate quantity of public goods for reasons discussed in Chapter 5.

Problem Solving Example:

Q How does the price system help allocative efficiency? Explain how prices can act as "feedback mechanisms" to offset the depletion of resources?

A The price system helps allocative efficiency by identifying the cheapest production processes and by reallocating resources. A firm, for example, can choose the most efficient combination of capital and labor by comparing the prices (and productivities) of capital and labor. These factor (capital and labor) prices are determined by the supplies of the factors, relative to the demand for the factors. Thus, in a country with an abundant population, but little capital, profit-maximizing firms will probably use relatively labor-intensive methods of production because the price of labor will be relatively low due to its abundance.

The scarcer factor of production and capital, will have a relatively higher price and will therefore be conserved and applied only in its most highly valued uses. This analysis of factor prices also applies to non-renewable natural resources. As, for example, oil becomes more scarce, its price rises. As its price climbs, there are two reactions. First of all, people tend to cut down on oil consumption; they try to curtail their use of oil so they do not have to spend so much of their incomes on it. In addition to conservation, they look for alternative energy sources. Thus, as the price of oil has climbed in the past few years, the search for other energy sources (coal, solar energy, etc.) has intensified.

The second reaction to the higher price is that firms now have incentives to expand output by drilling deeper, costlier wells, or, as is the case with other natural resources, by recycling them. So, the price mechanism automatically induces responses to alleviate shortages of resources. This tends to offset, and overrule, the rapid depletion of resources.

Prices, then, help determine the rate of growth by contributing to allocative efficiency, and by inducing consumers to economize on scarce resources. This tends to undermine predictions of economic collapse based on shortages of resources. Shortages will be reflected in higher prices, which will spur consumers and producers to use alternative resources.

4.6 Aptness of the Market Economy Model

Critics from all points on the political spectrum have criticized the market economy model as a description of both the structure and performance of the American economy.

From the standpoint of structure, some of the major problems they point out include:

1. The existence of gigantic firms and limitations on competition in many important markets.

2. The perceived widespread existence of externalities.

3. The size and intrusiveness of government.

4. Consumer and worker ignorance.

From the standpoint of performance, major problems they point to include:

1. Extended periods of high unemployment, high inflation, and sluggish growth.

2. The perception of dramatic inequality in income and wealth.

3. Anecdotal evidence of corruption, abuse of power, and wasteful practices in business.

Even supporters of the model admit that it is highly simplified. Students must decide for themselves whether the abstract model is insightful or misleading.

CHAPTER 5

The Private Sector of the American Economy

5.1 Private Sector

The private sector refers to households and privately-owned businesses.

5.2 Households

A household is defined as a group of people living in the same residence. Households are buyers of goods and services, savers and borrowers, and owners and suppliers of resources to firms. There are approximately 80,000,000 households in the United States.

5.3 Types of Business Organization

Firms—Business firms buy or rent resources, save and invest in capital equipment, and produce goods and services. There are approximately 16,000,000 firms in the United States.

Proprietorship—A proprietorship is a type of business where one individual owns and manages the firm and is solely and personally responsible for all debts incurred by the firm. Major advantages are that:

1. They are easy to establish.

2. The owner has absolute control over the direction the firm takes.

Disadvantages include:

1. Limitations on size—Proprietorships tend to be small because they must rely on the capital of only one individual and there are limits to how much one person can manage.

2. Unlimited liability—The full debt of the firm becomes the **personal** responsibility of the proprietor.

3. Limited life—The proprietorship dies when the owner dies.

There are approximately 11,000,000 proprietorships in the United States.

Partnership—A partnership is a type of business where two or more individuals own and manage a firm. Advantages of the partnership form are:

1. Easy to establish.

2. They tend to be larger than proprietorships because they draw on more than one source of capital and can employ cooperative management.

Disadvantages include:

1. Unlimited liability—Each partner is **personally** and **fully** liable for all debts of the business. If your partners skip out to Brazil, you may have to cover all the business debts.

2. Decision-making gets progressively harder as the number of partners increases.

3. Like the proprietorship, a partnership dies when any one of the partners die.

There are approximately 2,000,000 partnerships in the United States.

Corporation—A corporation is a type of business with characteristics established by law. Corporations must obtain a corporate charter from a state government. This charter provides the right to do business and gives the corporation many of the legal rights enjoyed by persons. Corporations raise their initial capital (and sometimes later infusions) by selling shares of stock. The stockholders (shareholders) become the owners of the corporation with ownership rights based on the amount of stock owned.

Advantages of the corporate form include:

1. Large size—There is virtually no limit to the amount of capital a corporation can raise.

2. Limited liability—Stockholders are liable for corporate debts only to the extent of their stock investment.

3. Unlimited life—Corporations can continue even if their initial owners die.

4. Legal rights—In the United States, corporations enjoy most of the legal rights of persons.

Disadvantages include:

1. Double taxation—Government taxes corporate profits directly and indirectly by taxing profit shares paid out to owners.

There are 3,000,000 corporations in the United States.

Conglomerate—A conglomerate is a business firm that competes in two or more unrelated industries.

Multinational—A multinational is a firm that has factories or offices in more than one country.

INDUSTRY

An industry is a group of firms that produce the same or a similar product. Some industries consist of only one firm.

Industrial Policy—Industrial policy refers to a wide variety of government policies that can be used to enhance or protect the productivity and competitive position of domestic industries and firms. Often a specific goal is to improve the ability of domestic industries or firms to withstand foreign competition or compete in foreign markets. Another common goal is to create more high-paying jobs and increase the rate of growth of the economy. Examples of these policies include protection against imports, government financial support for research and development, exemptions from antitrust restrictions, and government allocation of financial capital.

Problem Solving Example:

Q   What is the predominant form of business organization in the United States in terms of number of firms? What is the predominant form in terms of volume of output?

A   In terms of the number of firms, the sole proprietorship is overwhelmingly the predominant type of business organization. By 1973, about 78 percent of all American businesses were sole proprietorships.

In terms of volume of output, however, corporations easily produce more than any other type of business organization. Generally, corporations, constituting about 14 percent of all firms, produce about two-thirds of total business output.

ANTITRUST

Antitrust refers to a series of laws that attempt to promote greater competition in the private business sector.

5.4   Distribution of Income and Wealth

Wealth—Wealth is anything you own of value. What makes wealth valuable is that it provides to its owner goods, services, or money. Examples of wealth would be stocks and bonds, real estate, a bank account, education and work skills, farm animals, and artwork. The amount of wealth a person possesses is measured at a particular point in time. This makes wealth a stock variable.

STOCK VARIABLE

An economic variable that can only be meaningfully measured at a particular point in time.

Net Worth—An individual's net worth is the difference between the value of his/her wealth and his debts. It too is a stock variable.

Income—Income is the goods, services, or money that wealth provides. Examples of income are dividends and interest payments from stocks and bonds, the pleasures of living in your own house, interest payments and convenience from a bank account, wages and salaries from education and work skills, milk and meat from farm animals, and the enjoyment of viewing a great painting.

The amount of income a person receives is measured over a particular period of time, for example, a week, month, or year. This makes income a flow variable.

FLOW VARIABLE

An economic variable whose value can only be meaningfully measured over a period of time.

Some forms of income cannot be easily measured, such as the enjoyment from great paintings, and are typically excluded from analyses of people's incomes.

Compensation of Employees	**$2,904.7**
Proprietor's Income	**324.5**
Rent	**19.3**
Corporate Profits	**328.1**
Interest	**391.5**
National Income	**$3,968.1**

Source: *Survey of Current Business*
All figures in billions

Table 5.1 Functional Distribution of Income

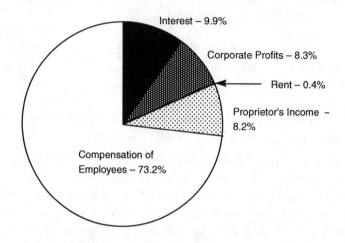

Figure 5.1 Functional Distribution of Income

Functional Distribution of Income—The functional distribution of income shows national income broken down by the type of resource that earned it (see Table 5.1 and Figure 5.1). Somewhat loosely, wages, rent, interest, proprietor's income, and corporate profits can be thought of as the returns to labor, land, capital, and entrepreneurship.

Personal Distribution of Income—The personal distribution of income shows the distribution among households (see Table 5.2). An obvious conclusion is that income is distributed far from equally in the United States.

Income Range	Percent of Households
<$2,500	2.3
$2,500–4,999	4.6
$5,000–7,499	6.3
$7,500–9,999	5.2
$10,000–12,499	5.6
$12,500–14,999	5.0
$15,000–19,999	10.0
$20,000–24,999	9.2
$25,000–34,999	16.1
$35,000–49,999	17.2
>$50,000	18.5

Median Household Income	$25,986
Mean Household Income	$32,144

Table 5.2 Personal Distribution of Income by Households

Trends in Median Family Income—At times in the last decade, median family income was $30,853. The graph shows family income adjusted for changes in the purchasing power of the dollar. After increasing on average 4.0 percent a year from 1947 to 1973, family income fell below the 1973 level of $30,820, not passing that level until 1987.

MEDIAN FAMILY INCOME

The median income is the one right in the middle. Half the families make more and half make less.

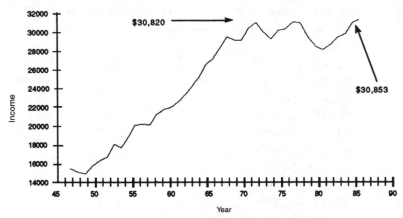

Figure 5.2 Trends in Median Family Income

POVERTY RATE

The poverty rate measures the proportion of the population that is considered poor. A person is considered poor if he/she lives in a household that receives less than a certain amount of money income for a household of that size. At times in the past decade, the poverty line for a household of 4 was $11,611.

Trends in the Poverty Rate—After falling fairly steadily from 1959 through 1973, the poverty rate turned back up. Only recently has the rate resumed a downward movement.

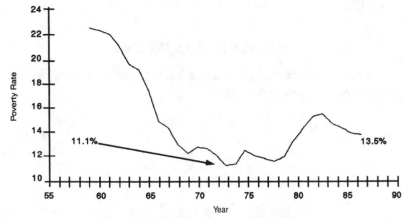

Figure 5.3 Trends in the Poverty Rate

The Distribution of Wealth—Wealth as measured by net worth is distributed unequally in the United States as Table 5.3 shows.

Net Worth	Percent of Families
<$5,000	33.0
$5,000–9,999	5.0
$10,000–24,999	12.0
$25,000–49,999	16.0
$50,000–99,999	17.0
$100,000–249,999	12.0
$250,000–499,999	3.0
>$500,000	2.0

Median Net Worth	$24,575
Mean Net Worth	$66,050

Source: *Federal Reserve Bulletin*

Table 5.3 Distribution of Family Net Worth

Problem Solving Example:

 Contrast the process of income distribution in capitalist vs. centrally planned economies.

In a capitalist economy, where the means of production are privately owned, the functional distribution of income among the various factors of production is determined by demand and supply in the factor markets. The wage rates, salaries, rents, and interest rates which firms are willing to pay for the services of each unit of labor, management, land, and capital, respectively, depend on its marginal revenue product, i.e., the value at the margin of its contribution to firms' sales revenues. In the market economy, firms' sales revenues depend on consumers' valuations of their products. Thus, the demand for factors tends to mirror consumers' implicit valuations of the contribution to output made by each factor. The quantity of each factor that will be supplied at any given price, on the other hand, depends on the valuations placed by owners of the factor on alternative uses of their resource (opportunity cost) relative to that price. The aggregate share of income (output) received by each factor of production in a capitalist market economy, then, is determined by the interplay of consumers' and factor owners' valuations of each factor, i.e., demand and supply, respectively.

In a centrally planned economy, on the other hand, there are no freely operating factor markets.

CHAPTER 6

The Public Sector of the American Economy

6.1 Public Sector

The public sector refers to the activities of government.

6.2 Government Spending

Government Expenditures on Goods and Services v. Transfer Payments—Government spending can be usefully broken down into two categories. One category is spending on goods and services. When government buys a battleship, a typewriter, or the Space Shuttle, it is acquiring goods. When government pays the salary of a soldier, teacher, or bureaucrat, it is getting a service in return. The second category is transfer payments. Transfers are money or in-kind items given to individuals or businesses for which the government receives no equivalent good or service in return. Examples would be social security payments, welfare, or unemployment compensation.

Functional Breakdown of Spending Side of Federal Budget—

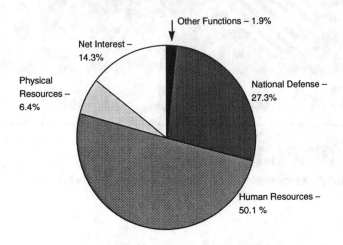

Figure 6.1 Federal Expenditures by Category

Functional Breakdown of Spending Side of State and Local Government Budgets—

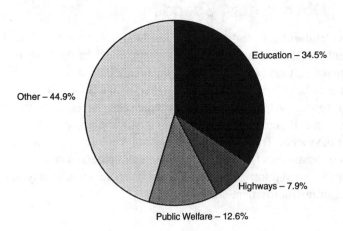

Figure 6.2 State and Local Government Spending by Category

Problem Solving Example:

 How are transfer payments different from government purchases?

When the government makes a purchase, it receives a good or service in return. Government purchases are often called exhaustive in that they directly absorb or employ resources, with the resultant production contributing to national output.

Transfer payments, on the other hand, are disbursements for which government currently receives no goods or services in return. Some examples of transfer payments are unemployment insurance and social security payments to the aged. Since transfer payments rechannel tax revenues back to households and businesses, they are in effect "negative taxes." Transfer payments are often called nonexhaustive because, as such, they do not directly absorb resources or account for production.

We can also distinguish between government purchases and transfer payments in the way they affect consumption of private and social goods. Being financed with tax money, government purchases tend to reallocate resources from private to social goods consumption. In the case of transfer payments, however, the tax money collected is rechanneled to other citizens. Therefore, there is no increase in social goods consumption here, but rather a change in the composition of private goods output. In this sense, transfer payments involve a lesser degree of government intervention in the economy than do government purchases.

6.3 Taxes

Average Tax Rate—The average tax rate (ATR) is the proportion of income paid in taxes.

$$\text{ATR} = \frac{\text{Taxes}}{\text{Income}}$$

Marginal Tax Rate—The marginal tax rate (MTR) is the proportion of each additional dollar paid in taxes.

$$MTR = \frac{\text{Taxes}}{\text{Income}}$$

Progressive Tax System—A progressive tax system is one where taxpayers with higher incomes pay a higher average tax rate. In the table, as income rises, not only are more taxes paid, but taxes are paid at a higher rate. An important feature of such a tax system is that the marginal tax rate increases as the level of income rises.

Taxable Income	20,000	22,000	24,000	26,000	28,000	30,000	32,000
Tax	2,000	2,300	2,700	3,200	3,800	4,500	5,300
ATR	.100	.105	.113	.123	.136	.150	.166
MTR	—	.150	.200	.250	.300	.350	.400

Proportional Tax System—A proportional tax system is one where all taxpayers pay the same average tax rate. In the table, as income rises, taxes paid increase, but taxes are paid at the same rate. An important feature of such a tax system is that the marginal tax rate is always equal to the average tax rate, and, consequently, remains the same as the level of income rises.

Taxable Income	20,000	22,000	24,000	26,000	28,000	30,000	32,000
Tax	3,000	3,300	3,600	3,900	4,200	4,500	4,800
ATR	.150	.150	.150	.150	.150	.150	.150
MTR	—	.150	.150	.150	.150	.150	.150

Regressive Tax System—A regressive tax system is one where taxpayers with higher incomes pay a lower average tax rate. In the table, as income rises, taxes paid rise but the average tax rate falls. An important feature of such a tax system is that the marginal tax rate decreases as the level of income rises.

Taxable Income	20,000	22,000	24,000	26,000	28,000	30,000	32,000
Tax	2,000	2,190	2,370	2,540	2,700	2,850	2,990
ATR	.100	.099	.098	.097	.096	.095	.093
MTR	—	.095	.090	.085	.080	.075	.070

User Charges—User charges are fees that individuals pay for the use of government services or to buy goods produced by government. Examples are entrance fees to national parks and charges for government documents purchased from the Government Printing Office.

6.4 Characteristics of a Good Tax

In addition to raising revenue, a good tax has the following characteristics:

Horizontal Equity—Horizontal equity is achieved when equals are treated equally, i.e., when individuals with similar circumstances are taxed the same.

Vertical Equity—Vertical equity is achieved when unequals are treated unequally, i.e., when individuals with different circumstances pay different amounts of tax.

Sources of Federal Tax Revenues—

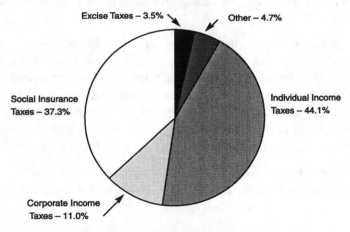

Figure 6.3 Sources of Federal Revenues

Sources of State and Local Government Tax Revenues—

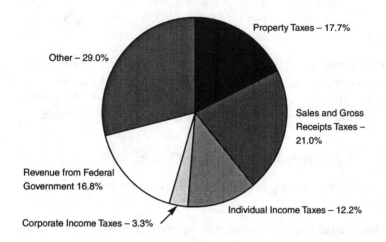

Property Taxes – 17.7%

Other – 29.0%

Sales and Gross
Receipts Taxes –
21.0%

Revenue from Federal
Government 16.8%

Corporate Income Taxes – 3.3%

Individual Income Taxes – 12.2%

Figure 6.4 Sources of State and Local Revenues

Incentives—If the allocation of resources yielded by a pure market system is considered ideal, then a good tax is one that would not change the actual allocation away from what the market would cause, or which would return the actual allocation to what the market would cause.

In the context of current American policy discussions, a good tax is one that does not adversely affect the decisions to work, save, and invest. Here the role of the marginal tax rate is considered crucial. The higher the marginal tax rate, the less an individual can keep out of any additional income earned. Consequently, a fear is that systems with marginal tax rates that are "too high" will lead to less work, saving, and investment, and a lower standard of living for that society.

Simplicity—Everything else held equal, systems that are easier to understand and require less effort to comply with are preferred.

Problem Solving Example:

Q What is the overall difference between federal taxes and state and local taxes? Explain.

A Federal taxes consist mainly of personal income taxes and corporate income taxes. The personal income tax is progressive and the corporation tax is only slightly progressive because there are only two rates, 22% on earnings up to $25,000 a year and 48% on all other earnings. Thus, federal taxes in total are mildly progressive.

State taxes consist mainly of retail sales taxes. Retail sales taxes are regressive because the spending of lower income groups consumes a larger part of their income than the spending of higher income groups. This regressive feature can be lessened by exempting food, fuel, medicine, and utilities from retail sales taxation.

Local tax systems rely mainly (for 86%) on property taxes. Because cheaper property tends to be overassessed in comparison with high-priced property, wealthier people are more likely to have influence with assessors or to threaten court action because of overassessment; and tenants usually have property taxes shifted to them as part of their rent; property taxes are considerably regressive. Thus, state and local taxes, due to general retail and property taxes, are slightly regressive.

6.5 Principles of Taxation

Benefit Principle—The benefit principle says that individuals should pay taxes in proportion to the benefits they receive from government. The problems with this principle include:

1. Not all taxpayers can afford the benefits they receive, e.g., welfare recipients.

2. Taxpayers have an incentive to understate the benefits they receive from government programs (the "free-rider" problem).

3. It is not an easy task to measure the benefits individuals receive from particular government programs, e.g., putting a monetary value on the benefits received from national defense.

Ability-to-Pay Principle—The ability-to-pay principle says that individuals should pay taxes based on their income or wealth (i.e., "ability-to-pay"). The rationale is that the most well-off have the most to lose if government does not function correctly. The problems with this principle include:

1. The equity issue of making people pay for services they do not receive.

2. The incentive problem associated with essentially penalizing people for being successful.

3. Determining the exact amount each person should pay.

Problem Solving Example:

 Distinguish between the two main principles of taxation.

The first main principle of taxation is the benefits principle. It holds that, as nearly as possible, the persons who benefit from a particular government service should pay the taxes to support that service. We can see the benefits principle roughly applied when we examine gasoline taxes. Here the costs of constructing and maintaining roads are met by a tax on each gallon of gasoline.

However, in other cases, it is not possible to apply the benefits principle. For example, it is difficult to quantify the benefit received by each individual from national defense. Would people living in an area more likely to be attacked benefit more than others? Would owners of large investments such as factories, which might be destroyed in a war, benefit more from defense than those who do not have such investments? If either were the case, according to the benefits principle, these persons ought to pay higher taxes. However, the difficulty in applying the benefits principle in this case is that it would be impossible to determine exact "quantities" of benefit and corresponding tax rates. Also, some citizens might actually suffer from national defense (those who live near air force bases and are annoyed by the noise of airplanes, for example). According to the benefits principle, the government should actually pay them.

The second main principle of taxation is the ability-to-pay principle. It holds that one's tax burden should be geared directly to one's financial position, i.e., tax would depend upon income, family size, situation in life, etc. The ability-to-pay principle is most readily realized through a tax on income itself, with some allowance for family size and such special circumstances as medical expenses.

6.6   Deficits, Surpluses, and the Public Debt

Budget Deficits—The government's budget is in deficit when its spending exceeds the amount of revenue brought in from taxes and user charges. To finance the spending in excess of revenues, the government borrows. The amount borrowed is equal to the deficit.

Budget Surpluses—The government's budget is in surplus when its spending is less than the amount of revenue brought in from taxes and user charges. The excess revenue can be used to pay back previous borrowing.

Public (National) Debt—The money government borrows to finance a deficit establishes the public's debt. Since the government has run more deficits than surpluses, the public debt has grown over time. Typically, government borrows money for long periods of time. Ten, twenty, and thirty year loans are not uncommon. These loans remain part of the public debt until they are paid. Even then, most loans that come due are paid back by borrowing from another source (refinancing) so, in a sense, the public debt is never paid back.

6.7   Role of Government

Public Goods and Services—Public goods and services have the following characteristics:

1. **Nonrival**—Consumption of the item by one person does not reduce the amount available for others to consume, or, equivalently, everyone can consume all of the item.

2. **Nonexclusion**—Nonpayers cannot be prevented from consuming the item.

The classic example of a public good is national defense. It is a nonrival good because the amount I consume on defense does not reduce the amount available for you to consume. We both consume our entire system of national defense. Also, national defense is nonexclusive. Assuming a system is in place, everyone in the country is protected, regardless of whether they have paid for it or not.

The opposite of a public good or service is a **private good or service**. The latter is both a rival and an exclusive good. It is rival because consumption by one reduces the amount available for all others, and it is exclusive because nonpayers can be prevented from consuming. A good example would be a soft drink. If I drink a can of soda, you cannot drink the same can. If you do not buy a can, you cannot enjoy the product.

Although a complete explanation would have to await microeconomics, economists believe that public goods will probably not be adequately supplied by the market. One of the main reasons stems from nonexclusion. Since you consume the good whether you pay or not, what is the incentive to pay? Consumers will rationally attempt to become "free riders," and the market would be unable to support a public good. Consequently, government is required to provide the good because government can do one thing the market cannot, it can compel people to pay. Also, and this point will be made without explanation, the nonrival characteristic implies that public goods and services should carry a price of $0, something that the market could obviously not support.

The existence of public goods and services provides a rationale for some government participation in the economy. The fact that government may be required to supply some goods and services does not imply government will always do a flawless job of it.

Merit Goods and Services—Merit goods and services are items that the government supplies because it thinks they are in the best interest of the public, whether the public demands the goods or not. An example is public television. It is highly unlikely that most of these shows could survive in the marketplace because there is not adequate viewer support.

Externalities—Externalities occur when a market transaction between two parties affects a third party who was not included in the transaction. An example would be if I buy a product from a producer whose production process pollutes the air that everyone breathes. The problem is that the effect on third parties is frequently ignored, to the detriment of third parties. Government action is frequently called for to rectify the damages to third parties or prevent the externality from happening. An example would be government regulation of pollution.

Conservative View of the Proper Role of Government—In the American context, a conservative in economic matters tends to believe the following:

1. The **performance**, if not structure, of our economy closely resembles that of a pure market economy.

2. The distribution of income and wealth is proportional to individual contributions to the economy, and hence, is quite equitable.

3. As a consequence, the need for government participation in the economy is quite limited.

4. Government is inherently inefficient and its actions are frequently inequitable.

5. Most of our major economic problems can be traced to misguided government policies. For example, inflation and recession is largely caused by mismanaged fiscal and monetary policy, unemployment largely reflects government policies that reduce wage flexibility, and sluggish growth is the result of too high tax rates and overregulation.

Liberal View of the Proper Role of Government—In the American context, a liberal in economic matters tends to believe the following:

1. Both in structure and performance, our economy does not resemble a pure market economy. Widespread monopoly and externalities and consumer and worker ignorance leads to inefficiency.

2. The distribution of income and wealth is distorted by economic power and widespread discrimination, and hence, cannot be considered equitable. In addition, strict adherence to a contributory standard in an economy characterized by a high degree of specialization and interdependence cannot be justified.

3. As a consequence, widespread government participation in the economy is required to fight monopoly and discrimination, protect consumers and workers, and redistribute income.

4. With the exercise of proper care, government is capable of successfully carrying out its duties.

5. Greater government intervention in the economy has led to better performance. Major economic problems are the result of too little government oversight, not too much.

Public Choice—Public Choice is one of the newest fields within the discipline of economics. It applies economic methodology to analyze the actions of governments, politicians, and bureaucrats.

Quiz: Economic Systems—The Public Sector of the American Economy

1. Which of the following is not a distinguishing feature of capitalism?

    (A) Freedom of enterprise

    (B) Government control of industry

    (C) Freedom of consumer choice

    (D) Competition

2.   The circular flow model of capitalism illustrates

    (A) how the prices of resources, goods, and services are determined.

    (B) how competition achieves economic efficiency under capitalism.

    (C) how resources are allocated.

    (D) how households and firms interact through markets.

3.   Consumer sovereignty means that

    (A) consumers are protected from fraud by the government.

    (B) the government is the primary consumer of goods and services in the economy.

    (C) the state directs the production of consumer goods.

    (D) consumers ultimately determine what goods are produced.

4.   Of the following, which are advantages to a single proprietor?

    (A) Unlimited liability

    (B) Mutual agency

    (C) Ease in obtaining funds

    (D) Control over decisions

5.   An advantage of a partnership over a single proprietorship is

    (A) limited liability.

    (B) greater specialization of management.

    (C)   less "red tape" in forming the business.

    (D)   unlimited liability.

6.   Which of the following is not true of a corporation?

    (A)   Unlimited liability

    (B)   Ease in obtaining funds

    (C)   Lower tax rate on corporate income than on personal income

    (D)   Greater efficiency brought about by greater size

7.   The marginal tax rate is

    (A)   the decrease in taxes paid as additional income is obtained.

    (B)   the ratio of total taxes paid to total income.

    (C)   the increase in taxes paid as additional income is obtained, divided by that increase in income.

    (D)   the total tax rate less the average tax rate.

8.   A tax structure is said to be progressive if

    (A)   the tax rate remains the same, regardless of the size of income.

    (B)   the tax increases the total volume of consumer expenditures.

    (C)   the tax rate increases as income increases.

    (D)   the tax rate declines as income increases.

9.   Which one of the following relates directly to the benefits-received principle of taxation?

    (A)   Progressive tax rates

    (B)   Proportional tax rates

(C)   Federal excise tax on alcoholic beverages

(D)   Personal income tax

10.   The ability-to-pay philosophy is most evident in

(A)   an excise tax on coffee.

(B)   an excise tax on gasoline.

(C)   a tax on residential property.

(D)   a progressive income tax.

ANSWER KEY

1.	(B)	6.	(A)
2.	(D)	7.	(C)
3.	(D)	8.	(C)
4.	(D)	9.	(C)
5.	(B)	10.	(D)

CHAPTER 7

Gross National Product

7.1 Measuring GNP

Gross National Product—Gross National Product (or GNP) is a measure of the dollar value of final goods and services produced by the economy over a given period of time, usually one year. It is the most comprehensive indicator of the economy's health available, although it is not a measure of society's overall well-being.

Final Goods and Services—Final goods and services are those sold to their ultimate users.

Intermediate Goods and Services—Intermediate goods and services are those in an intermediate stage of processing. They are purchased by firms for immediate resale, such as the frozen orange juice a grocery store buys from the processor for resale to consumers or they are purchased for further processing and then resale, such as the crude oil a refinery buys to refine into gasoline and other petroleum products.

GNP in the Circular Flow—Assume a simple economy composed of three business firms and one household. Firm A manufactures computer chips. It takes silicon from the environment (assumed to be so plentiful as to be a free good) and combines it with resources purchased or rented from the household. The resulting chips are sold to Firm B, a manufacturer of computers. Firm B takes the chips and combines them with the resources purchased from the household to produce computers which it sells to Firm C, a retail computer store. The store uses resources obtained from the household to resell the computers to the household, which is the ultimate user.

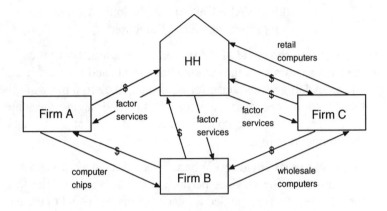

Figure 7.1 GNP in the Circular Flow

The table traces the transactions that take place in the economy during the course of a year.

Firm	Cost of Intermediate Goods Purchased	Cost of Resources Purchased	Goods Sold	Value-Added
A	0	50	50	50
B	50	75	125	75
C	125	40	165	40

Table 7.1

There are three ways to measure GNP.

1. **Expenditures on Final Goods and Services**—In the example, computer chips and wholesale computers are intermediate goods

while retail computers are a final good. Since the household spent $165 on retail computers, this is a direct measure of GNP.

2. **Sum of Value-Added for All Firms—**

Value-Added (VA) = Cost of Goods Sold – Cost of
Intermediate Goods Purchased

VA measures the value of the processing and resale activities that the firm performs on the intermediate goods and services it purchases. Adding value-added for all firms in the economy will give GNP. It follows because the value of final goods and services produced results from the contributions of all firms at all stages of the production process.

3. **Gross National Income**—Where does value-added come from? It comes from the services performed by the resources the firms hire. Therefore, value-added for each firm is just equal to the payments made for resources allowing us to total the incomes earned by all households to get GNP. This measure is frequently given the name Gross National Income (or GNI).

Trends in GNP—GNP rose from $91.3 billion in 1939 to $4,864.3 billion in the past decade.

Problem Solving Example:

Define Gross National Product (GNP).

Gross National Product, otherwise known as GNP, is defined as the total market value of all final goods and services produced in the economy in one year. An important clarification has to be made here. All goods produced in a particular year may not be sold: some may be added to inventories. Nevertheless, any increase in inventories must be included in determining GNP, since GNP measures all current production regardless of whether or not it is sold.

7.2 Nominal versus Real Values

A nation's GNP is measured in terms of its national currency. In the United States, GNP is measured in dollars. The reason is to have a common unit to measure disparate goods. It is impossible to add 10 bushels of apples and 30 crates of oranges, but we can add $60 of apples and $100 of oranges. What this means is we must compute the market value of each good or service produced.

Market Value = Market Price of Good or Service × Quantity

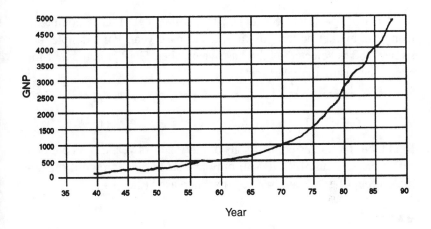

Figure 7.2 Trends in GNP

Nominal GNP—Nominal GNP (or current dollar GNP or money GNP) is GNP computed by using the current year's market price for each product. For example, nominal GNP is computed using the quantity produced of each good or service and the price each good or service sold for during the year.

$$GNP^{89} = P_1^{89} \times Q_1^{89} + P_2^{89} \times Q_2^{89} + \ldots + P_n^{89} \times Q_n^{89}$$

where the subscripts refer to all the different goods and services produced, and the superscripts refer to the year.

Use of nominal GNP can create problems when comparing GNP across time. Consider GNP^{89} compared to GNP^{80}.

$$GNP^{80} = P_1^{80} \times Q_1^{80} + P_2^{80} \times Q_2^{80} + \ldots + P_n^{80} \times Q_n^{80}$$

$$GNP^{89} = P_1^{89} \times Q_1^{89} + P_2^{89} \times Q_2^{89} + \ldots + P_n^{89} \times Q_n^{89}$$

Presumably, the purpose of GNP comparisons is to see whether GNP has grown, or, more exactly, whether the economy's output of goods and services has increased (the Q's). Yet GNP could have grown between 1980 and 1989 just due to increases in prices (the P's).

Real GNP—Real GNP (or constant dollar GNP) is GNP computed using the market prices from a selected base year. For example, assume 1980 is selected as the base year. Then GNP is computed for every year using the 1980 prices.

$$GNP^{80} = P_1^{80} \times Q_1^{80} + P_2^{80} \times Q_2^{80} + \ldots + P_n^{80} \times Q_n^{80}$$

$$GNP^{89} = P_1^{80} \times Q_1^{89} + P_2^{80} \times Q_2^{89} + \ldots + P_n^{80} \times Q_n^{89}$$

Real GNP facilitates comparisons of GNP across years. If a common set of prices is used, GNP will only appear to have grown if the actual output of goods and services has increased (the Q's).

EXAMPLE

	Bread			Soda Pop			
	P	Q	PQ	P	Q	PQ	GNP
Nominal^{80}	2.00	150	300	1.00	500	500	800
Nominal^{89}	2.20	200	440	1.10	600	660	1,100
Real^{89}	2.00	200	400	1.00	600	600	1,000

Table 7.2

BASE YEAR

A base year is an arbitrarily chosen year which is used as the basis of comparison in an analysis.

GNP Deflator—The GNP deflator is a measure of the average price level in a given year. The GNP deflator for the base year is always given the value 100. The deflator for earlier and later years is proportionately scaled up or down based on the percentage change in the average price level. For example, if the deflator was 108 in the year after the base year, the average level of prices would have risen by 8 percent.

$$\text{GNP Deflator}^{xx} = (\text{Nominal GNP}^{xx}/\text{Real GNP}^{xx}) \times 100$$

Using the data from the table:

$$\text{GNP Deflator}^{89} = (1{,}100/1{,}000) \times 100 = 110$$

The GNP deflator can be used to "deflate" nominal GNP data into real terms.

$$\text{Real GNP}^{xx} = (\text{Nominal GNP}^{xx}/\text{GNP Deflator}^{xx}) \times 100$$

Using the data from the table:

$$\text{Real GNP}^{89} = (1{,}100/110) \times 100 = 1{,}000$$

Problem Solving Example:

What happens to the purchasing power of money when there is inflation? What does it mean?

The purchasing power of money is the real value of money, i.e., what you can buy for each dollar. Nominal GNP is the sum of the products of the quantities of goods purchased times their prices:

$$\text{nominal GNP} = P_1Q_1 + P_2Q_2 + P_3Q_3 + \ldots + P_nQ_n.$$

It is also equal to real GNP times the GNP-deflator: nominal GNP = real GNP × deflator = Q × P. The deflator is the general price level. From the exchange equation we know that nominal GNP = P × Q = M × V, where M is the quantity of money supplied and v is the velocity of the money turnover, i.e., the frequency with which money changes hands. Suppose the quantity of money supplied and the velocity do not change over time, so that nominal GNP is constant. Then when there is inflation and the general price level P creeps up, real income = real GNP decreases, $\overline{MV}$ = constant = P ↑ × Q ↓, and less goods can be purchased with the same amount of money.

7.3 Problems with Measuring GNP

Market v. Non-market Production—Since GNP measures the market value of final goods and services, only those goods and services that have been sold in markets can be included in GNP. This excludes a significant amount of our nation's production. Examples of excluded production would be the produce of backyard vegetable gardens, the home services performed by homemakers, all do-it-yourself activities, and criminal activity.

Secondhand Goods—GNP is a measure of our current production of goods and services. This means sales of already produced items, such as used cars, are not included.

Assets—GNP does not measure the value of our national and personal assets.

GNP as a Measure of Social Welfare—GNP is only a measure of production. While goods and services certainly contribute to human happiness, they are not all that is needed. GNP does not measure the value of the love, caring and friendship in society, or take account of available leisure. Also, it includes some production that arguably does not lead to greater happiness. For example, if there is a crime wave and society produces more burglar alarms, GNP will go up although society is probably not better off.

Problem Solving Example:

GNP attempts to measure the annual production of the economy. Non-productive transactions should not be included in its computation. What are "non-productive transactions"?

Non-productive transactions are of two major types:

1. purely financial transactions

2. secondhand sales

Purely financial transactions include public and private transfer payments and trade in securities.

Transfer payments do not entail production but simply the transfer of funds (as opposed to wage payment) from the government to individuals.

Stock market transactions involve merely the swapping of claims to real assets; these transactions do not involve current production.

Secondhand sales either reflect no current production, or they involve double counting, because the production of the particular good has already taken place, and its value should not be included in (current) GNP.

7.4   Components of GNP and GNI

Components of GNP and GNI

GNP

Personal Consumption Expenditures	$3,227.5
Gross Private Domestic Investment	766.5
Government Purchases of Goods and Services	964.9
Net Exports	−94.6
	$4,864.3

GNI

Compensation of Employees	$2,904.7
Proprietor's Income	324.5
Rent	19.3
Corporate Profits	328.1
Interest	391.5
Capital Consumption Allowance	506.3
Indirect Business Taxes	389.9
	$4,864.3

Personal Consumption Expenditures (C)—This category includes all spending by households, with the exception of purchases of new homes. An interesting inclusion is the imputed value of owner-occupied housing, one of the few examples of non-market production in GNP.

Gross Private Domestic Investment (I)—This category includes private business spending for new capital equipment, changes in business inventories, and household purchases of new homes.

Why Gross Investment?—Investment spending can take place to replace capital goods that have worn out (called replacement investment) or to add to the stock of capital goods (called net investment). Gross investment is the sum of replacement and net.

Why "Changes in Inventory"?—Inventory refers to already produced goods that are being stored in anticipation of later sale. Changes in inventory are included in GNP to allow us to distinguish production from sales and get an accurate measure of GNP.

Assume on January 1 businesses hold inventories of $80 billion, consisting of goods that were produced in the past but unsold. Assume further that during the year $5 trillion of final goods and services were produced, but only $4.9 trillion of these were sold. The unsold $100 billion goes into inventory so on December 31, inventories stand at $180 billion. The correct measure of GNP is $5,000 billion, but if we only measure sales we will fall short. Consequently, we must add the **change** in inventories ($180 billion – $80 billion = $100 billion) to the sales to get an accurate count of GNP.

Inv = $80 bill   produce $5 trillion   Inv = $180 bill

Jan. 1   sell $4.9 trillion   Dec. 31

Government Spending on Goods and Services (G)—All government (federal, state, and local) purchases of goods and services are included in this category. This does not include transfer payments, since transfers do not signify current production.

Net Exports of Goods and Services (X – M)—Net Exports = Exports (X) – Imports (M). Even though our nation does not get to consume the goods and services we sell to foreign countries, exports are included because they are part of our production. Imports are included under consumption but must be subtracted here because they do not represent our production. International flows of assets are not included here.

Compensation of Employees—This category includes all wages, salaries, and supplements. Supplements are aspects of employee compensation that do not show up in the paycheck, such as employer contributions to social security.

Rent—This category includes landlord incomes and sundry other items.

Interest—This category measures the income earned from lending money.

Proprietor's Income—The income earned by businesses that are not corporations is proprietor's income.

Corporate Profits—The profits of corporations.

Indirect Business Taxes—These are taxes paid by business that are not levied on sales or income. Examples would be property taxes and license fees.

Capital Consumption Allowances—This is an estimate of the value of capital depreciation in the economy.

DEPRECIATION

Capital goods "wear down" with use or time. Depreciation is an estimate of this reduction in value and is a cost of production.

Problem Solving Example:

What is the difference between gross national product and national income?

Gross National Product (GNP) is the dollar value of all goods and services produced in a year in the United States. National Income (NI), which is the total income earned by those who contribute to current production, represents the GNP remaining after deductions are made for indirect taxes, depreciation, and the use of capital.

7.5   Other Measures of Income

Net National Product—

Gross National Product	$4,864.3
– Capital Consumption Allowances	–506.3
Net National Product	$4,358.0

NNP measures current production of goods and services less any replacement investment. Since replacement investment does not measure "forward progress" for the economy, NNP may be conceptually a superior measure of the state of the economy than GNP. Since Capital Consumption Allowance data is such a crude estimate of actual depreciation, NNP is not widely used.

National Income—

Net National Product	$4,358.0
− Indirect Business Taxes	−389.9
National Income	$3,968.1

(figures may not add up due to rounding)

NI measures the income earned by factors of production.

Personal Income—

National Income	$3,968.1
− Income earned but not received	−1,164.3
+ Income received but not earned	+1,258.2
Personal Income	$4,062.0

Examples of income earned but not received would be employer supplements to wages and salaries and some payroll taxes. Income taxes are not subtracted here (although they fit the definition). An example of income received but not earned would be transfer payments to households. An advantage of personal income is that data is available monthly.

Disposable Income—

Personal Income	$4,062.1
− Personal Taxes	−590.3
Disposable Income	$3,471.8

DI is the income households have available to spend or save as they please.

CHAPTER 8

Macroeconomic Problems

of the American Economy

8.1 The Business Cycle

Business Cycles—Business cycles are the alternating periods of prosperity and recession that seem to characterize all market-oriented economies.

Four Phases of the Cycle—Every business cycle consists of four phases. The peak is the high point of business activity. It occurs at a specific point in time. The contraction is a period of declining business activity. It occurs over a period of time. The trough is the low point in business activity. It too occurs at a specific point in time. The expansion is a period of growing business activity. It takes place over a period of time.

Although the word cycle implies a certain uniformity, that is misleading. Each business cycle differs from every other in terms of duration of contractions and expansions, and height of peak and depth of trough.

Seasonal Fluctuations—Seasonal fluctuations are changes in economic variables that reflect the season of the year. For example, every summer ice cream sales soar. They decrease during winter. Every December, toy sales increase dramatically. They fall back during January.

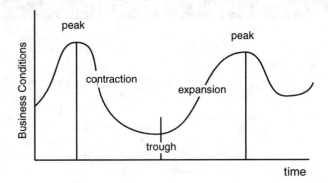

Figure 8.1 Phases of the Business Cycle

Secular Trends—A secular trend is the long run direction of movement of a variable. For example, our economy has become dramatically richer over the past century. We can say that there was a secular upward trend in real GNP. Of course, growth was not steady. There were periods of faster than average followed by slower than average growth, which accounts for business cycles.

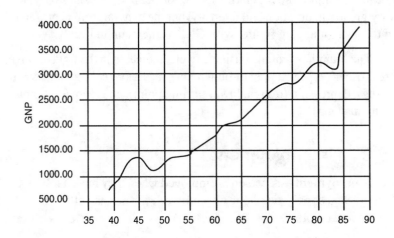

Figure 8.2 Secular Trend and Cycle in Real GNP

Problem Solving Example:

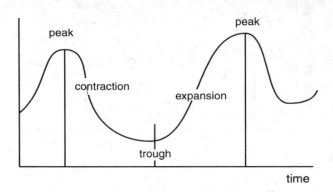

 What are "business cycles" or "business fluctuations"?

The term "business cycles" refers to variations in the level of economic activity over a period of years. Some economists prefer the term "business fluctuations," rather than business cycles, because it implies no regularity, as the former does. Business "cycles" vary greatly in duration and intensity, but the general form is presented in the accompanying figure, with GNP as the main indicator.

The four phases of the business cycle, indicated in the figure above, are prosperity (peak, upper turning point), recession (contraction, downswing), depression (trough, lower turning point), and recovery (expansion, upswing).

8.2 Unemployment

Employment—A person is employed when they have a job. In the United States, only one hour of paid work a week is sufficient to be considered employed.

Unemployment—People are considered unemployed when they are without a job and **actively seeking** one. Active seeking includes such behaviors as reading want ads, contacting employers, and using the services of the public employment agencies.

Labor Force—The labor force consists of all people who have a job or would like a job and are actively seeking one. In short, the labor force consists of all employed and unemployed people.

Labor Force Participation Rate—The labor force participation rate (LFPR) is the percentage of the population in the labor force.

$$\text{LFPR} = \frac{\text{Labor Force}}{\text{Population}}$$

Unemployment Rate—The unemployment rate is the number of unemployed people as a percentage of the **labor force**.

$$\text{Unemployment Rate} = \frac{\text{Unemployed}}{\text{Labor Force}}$$

Employment Rate—The employment rate is the number of employed people as a percentage of the **population**.

$$\text{Employment Rate} = \frac{\text{Employed}}{\text{Population}}$$

Full Employment—Full employment is not a situation where the employment is 100%, or the unemployment rate is 0%. There is some unemployment at full employment. While no one can say for sure what the full employment unemployment rate is, most economists believe full employment is obtained when the unemployment rate is in the 4-5.5% range. At full employment, the number of vacant jobs is just equal to the number of unemployed people. The unemployed just have not located the jobs or lack the required skills. Since there is no shortage or surplus of labor, wages should remain stationary at full employment.

Natural Rate of Unemployment—The natural rate of unemployment can be defined in three equivalent ways:

1. It is the level of unemployment at which the expected rate of inflation equals the actual rate,

2. It is the level of unemployment at which the labor market is in equilibrium, and

3. It is "true" full employment.

Frictional Unemployment—The frictionally unemployed are workers who are "between jobs." These are workers who have quit, been fired, been laid off due to a decline in a firm or industry, or just entered the labor force. They likely will find a new job in a reasonable amount of time, but they have not found one yet. Some frictional unemployment is to be expected since labor market information (location of job vacancies, characteristics of job, etc.) tends to be limited. Frictional unemployment is found at full employment, but its level is influenced by the availability of job market information.

Structural Unemployment—The structurally unemployed are workers who lack the skills to fill available job vacancies. Some structural unemployment is inevitable in a dynamic economy. Structural unemployment is found at full employment, but its level could be influenced by the availability of retraining opportunities.

Cyclical Unemployment—The cyclically unemployed are workers who have lost their jobs due to a downturn in the business cycle.

Discouraged Workers—Discouraged workers are people who are without a job, want a job, but have looked unsuccessfully for such a long time that they have, in effect, "given up" the search. Officially, they are counted as "not in the labor force" because they are not actively seeking work, but they do want a job. During deep recessions and in some areas of the countries at all times, the number of discouraged workers can be considerable.

Problem Solving Examples:

What are frictional, structural, and cyclical unemployment?

Frictional unemployment occurs as workers change jobs. Structural unemployment occurs when workers become unemployed because the industry is replacing workers by machines or reducing the number of employees because of an increase in the efficiency of use of labor.

Economists consider frictional and structural unemployment to be more or less unavoidable since workers are free to choose employment and to search for a job, and the modern industrial economy fosters and encourages technological advancement.

Cyclical unemployment occurs when the economy is for some reason producing at a lower level than that desired by society. The economy in general does not have jobs for all those who are able and willing to work because aggregate demand is deficient; cyclical unemployment occurs in the recession phase of the business cycle.

What is natural unemployment and what are its determinants?

The natural rate of unemployment is that rate of unemployment at which flows in and out of unemployment just balance, and at which expectations of firms and workers as to the behavior of prices and wages are correct (see figure below).

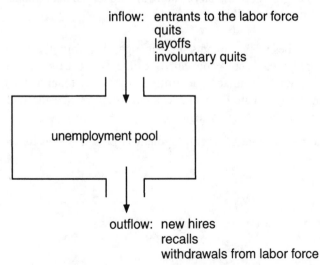

inflow: entrants to the labor force
quits
layoffs
involuntary quits

unemployment pool

outflow: new hires
recalls
withdrawals from labor force

The determinants of the natural rate of unemployment are grouped under the duration and frequency of unemployment.

The duration of unemployment is the average period of time to find and accept a job, after entry into the pool of unemployed. It depends on:

1. The organization of the labor market, its informational structure, in regard to the presence or absence of employment agencies, youth employment services, etc.;

2. The demographic make-up of the labor force (males vs. females; whites vs. non-whites; various age groups);

3. The ability and desire of the unemployed to keep looking for a better job; and

4. The availability and type of jobs.

The two basic determinants of the frequency of unemployment are:

1. The variability of demand for labor across different firms in the economy: some firms are growing and some are contracting. The higher this variability, the higher the natural unemployment rate will be.

2. The rate at which new workers enter the labor force: the faster the growth of the labor force, the higher the natural unemployment rate will be.

All of these determinants may change; therefore, the natural rate of unemployment is not a constant over time. Because the natural rate of unemployment is primarily determined by institutional arrangements and not by aggregate demand, it is considered to be the rate corresponding to "full" employment.

The natural rate of unemployment is presently considered to be 5.5%.

8.3 Inflation

Inflation—Inflation is a sustained, substantial increase in the average level of prices.

Deflation—Deflation is a sustained, substantial decrease in the average level of prices.

Disinflation—Disinflation refers to a decrease in the rate of inflation.

Stagflation—Stagflation refers to a period of time when both the unemployment and inflation rates are high.

Hyperinflation—Hyperinflation refers to a period of extremely rapid inflation.

Consumer Price Index—Sometimes called the Cost of Living Index, the Consumer Price Index (or CPI) attempts to measure the cost of living for a typical family.

The initial step in constructing the CPI is to define a "market basket" of goods and services. The market basket is a representative sample of the goods and services that a typical family would buy over a given period of time. The cost of the market basket can be computed at different points in time. Changes in the cost of the market basket are taken to measure changes in the cost of living. Typically, the cost of the market basket is expressed in price index terms. The cost is given the arbitrary value of 100 in the arbitrarily chosen base year. The index is then scaled up or down proportionally in earlier or later periods of time.

	YEAR 1		YEAR 2	
	P	Cost	P	Cost
50 loaves of bread	2.00	100.00	2.10	105.00
100 bottles of soda	1.00	100.00	1.10	110.00
		200.00		215.00

Table 8.1

Constructing the Consumer Price Index

In Table 8.1, the market basket consists of 50 loaves of bread and 100 bottles of soda pop. In Year 1, they cost $2.00 per loaf and $1.00 per bottle, respectively, for a total cost of $200. In Year 2, the prices of both products and, consequently, the market basket rise. The new market basket cost of $215 is 7.5% greater than in Year 1 (($215 − $200)/$200 =. 075). Therefore, we conclude that the cost of living rose 7.5% between Year 1 and Year 2.

In index number terms, if we let the $200 cost in Year 1 be represented by 100, then the $215 will be represented by 107.5. The price index for Year 2 can be found by solving a ratio problem.

$$\frac{\text{Year 2}}{\text{Year 1}} = \frac{\$215}{\$200} = \frac{x}{100},$$

where x is the unknown index number for Year 2 and 100 is the base year index.

Index Number Mathematics

One use of the CPI is to "deflate" nominal consumer incomes into their equivalent in purchasing power:

$$\text{Purchasing Power of Income} = \left(\frac{\text{Nominal Income}}{\text{CPI}}\right) \times 100$$

For example, assume a consumer's nominal income was $30,000 in Year 1, our base year. Because it is the base year, the $30,000 is taken to have a purchasing power of $30,000 (($30,000/100) × 100). Assume the consumer's income rises to $34,000 in Year 2. Does this necessarily mean the consumer's purchasing power has risen by $4,000 or 13.34%? Can the consumer buy 13.34% more goods and services than she did in Year 1? If the prices rose between the two years, then the answer must be no. The nominal increase in Year 2 has a purchasing power of $31,627.91 (($34,000/107.5) × 100), which is only 5.43% greater than in Year 1. The interpretation of this result is that because of higher prices, $34,000 in Year 2 could only buy as much as $31,627.91 in Year 1.

Problems with the CPI—The CPI should be recognized as only a rough measure of the cost of living.

1. The index is constructed for the "typical family." Since no family is typical, the index will be inaccurate. For example, if your family normally consumes 45 loaves of bread and 110 bottles of soda, your cost of living would increase more than the index indicates because you are consuming relatively more of the item whose cost has increased relatively more.

	Year 1		Year 2	
	P	Cost	P	Cost
45 loaves of bread	$2.00	$ 90.00	$2.10	$ 94.50
110 bottles of soda	$1.00	$110.00	$1.10	$121.00
		$200.00		$215.50

Table 8.2

$$\text{CPI} = \frac{\$215.50}{\$200.00} = \frac{x}{100} \text{ , where } x = 107.75 \text{ in Year 2}$$

Construction of CPI for an Atypical Family

2. The index does not take into account the fact that people will alter their market basket in response to changes in prices. For example, if soda increased more than bread, people may respond by purchasing less of the relatively more expensive soda and more of the relatively cheaper bread.

3. The market basket is not adjusted for changes in the quality of products. Some price increases may simply reflect that the product is of higher quality.

4. The market basket is not continually altered to take into account the introduction of new products.

Redistribution of Income and Wealth—A serious problem caused by inflation is capricious redistribution of income and wealth. What is often not appreciated is the following. For every buyer, there is a seller, and every buyer is also a seller. If inflation causes buyers to pay 10% more for products, the same inflation will cause sellers to receive 10% more income. Consequently, society's income in the aggregate must keep pace with price changes. Unfortunately, there are some individuals whose income will lag behind price changes. As a result, they will be made worse off. There must be some whose income rises faster than inflation and are made better off. (Of course, they will think their increase in well-being is simply a reflection of their hard work and virtue.)

It is understandable that during periods of inflation, people desire to protect the purchasing power of their income. A common tactic of unionized workers is to demand **cost-of-living** escalators in wage contracts. A **cost-of-living** escalator is a clause requiring that wages be raised automatically as the cost-of-living rises. These escalators are sometimes called **COLA's** for **cost-of-living adjustments**. Another term is that wages are **indexed** to the cost-of-living. Currently, Federal Social Security recipients have their benefits indexed to the cost-of-living.

With respect to wealth, individuals who store their wealth in forms whose value does not keep pace with inflation will end up worse off. Money holders are particularly susceptible to inflation problems.

The following example illustrates the problem faced by lenders of money during inflationary times. Assume A (the lender or "creditor") loans $100.00 to B (the borrower or "debtor") for one year at 5% interest. A then is willing to sacrifice $100 in purchasing power for a year in the expectation of having $105.00 (the repaid principal of $100 plus the 5% interest) in purchasing power available in a year. Now assume there is 10% inflation during the year (the price index rises from 100 on January 1 to 110 on December 31). The $105.00 repaid will only have a purchasing power of $95.45 (($105.00/110) × 100). In effect, A will have lost because he/she was repaid less purchasing power than she expected to receive, and B gained because his/her cost of borrowing (in terms of purchasing power) was less than expected. Table 8.3 summarizes the discussion.

	No Inflation			Inflation		
	Nominal Amount	Purchasing Power	Price Index	Nominal Amount	Purchasing Power	Price Index
lent, beginning of year	$100.00	$100.00	100	$100.00	$100.00	100
repaid, end of year	$105.00	$105.00	100	$105.00	$ 95.45	110

Table 8.3

Is there any way for the creditor to protect himself/herself? What if the creditor could anticipate the inflation and added the 10% rate to the rate of interest charged? As the table shows, charging 15% interest would allow him/her to receive back approximately the amount of purchasing power he/she had initially expected. Assuming the debtor also anticipated 10% inflation, she would not resist paying a 15% interest rate because the terms of the loan would be no different than what she would have agreed to with no inflation. Thus, to protect their wealth, creditors will add the expected rate of inflation to the rate of interest they charge. This helps explain why interest rates tend to rise during periods of inflation. Of course, forecasting the rate of inflation is extremely difficult to do, so inflation has a tendency to increase uncertainty which may limit lending and borrowing.

Lender Charges 15% Interest

	Nominal Amount	Purchasing Power	Price Index
lent, beginning of year	$100.00	$100.00	100
repaid, end of year	$115.00	$104.55	110

Table 8.4

Inefficiencies—Inflation can also lead to inefficiency which can reduce national output and the rate of real growth. One source of problems is that an inflationary environment is typically one of great uncertainty. Prices and costs in the future cannot be known, and, consequently, long-term planning is disrupted. The impact of this is to reduce investment. Another problem is that the pattern of investment is frequently altered away from productive uses to those that are less productive, but may be a good inflation hedge. For example, speculation in gold and great art is common during inflationary times. A third problem is that people pay inordinate attention to their financial affairs, robbing themselves of time that could be used more productively.

Problem Solving Example:

 A rise in the general price level is called _____. How is this change measured?

 A rise in the general price level is called inflation and it is usually measured with the help of three indices:

1. the consumer price index (CPI);

2. the wholesale price index (WPI), which are both published by the Bureau of Labor Statistics; and

3. the GNP deflator, published by the Department of Commerce.

The CPI or WPI is the ratio of today's cost of a basket of goods of fixed composition. If we denote the base year quantities of the various goods by q_0^i and their base year prices by p_0^i, the cost of the basket in the base year is

$$\sum p_0^i q_0^i$$

where the summation (Σ) is over all goods in the basket. The cost of a basket of the same quantities but at today's prices is

$$\sum p_1^i q_0^i$$

where p_1^i is today's price. Then the price index =

$$\frac{\sum p_1^i q_0^i}{\sum p_0^i q_0^i} \times 100.$$

The GNP deflator is the ratio of the nominal GNP to the real GNP

$$p = \frac{\text{nominal GNP}}{\text{real GNP}}$$

so that real GNP is nominal GNP deflated

$$\text{real GNP} = \frac{\text{nominal GNP}}{p}$$

Quiz: Gross National Product— Macroeconomic Problems of the American Economy

1. GNP is not a very good measure of economic welfare because

   (A) it is a monetary measure.

   (B) it takes into account pollution and abatement services.

   (C) the expenditures and income approaches to GNP yield different results because the units of measurement are not the same.

   (D) it does not include nonmonetized activities.

2. National income or product means

   (A) the amount of money received by the people over an interval of time.

   (B) the money measure of the overall flow of final goods and services over an interval of time.

(C)   the total amount of money.

(D)   the income of the government over an interval of time.

3.   Real GNP and nominal GNP are similar in the sense that

(A)   real GNP and nominal GNP are both adjusted for changes in the price level.

(B)   they refer to all economic activities, monetized and nonmonetized.

(C)   they determine the market value of all monetized goods and services produced in an economy, usually for a year.

(D)   they are good measures of the distribution of resources in the world economy.

4.   NNP is

(A)   GNP adjusted for depreciation charges.

(B)   national income plus corporate income taxes.

(C)   NI minus indirect business taxes.

(D)   NI plus personal income and disposable income.

5.   Personal income equals disposable income plus

(A)   personal income taxes.

(B)   personal savings.

(C)   dividend payments.

(D)   payroll taxes.

6.   An important difference between personal income and personal disposable income consists of

(A)   dividends.

(B)   consumption expenditures.

(C) personal savings.

(D) personal income taxes.

7. Which of the following is not a phase of the business cycle?

(A) Recession

(B) Expansion

(C) Inflection

(D) Peak

8. The secular trend refers to

(A) fluctuations in business activity which average 40 months in duration.

(B) fluctuations in business activity which occur around Christmas, Easter, and so forth.

(C) fluctuations in business activity which average eight or nine years in duration.

(D) the long-term expansion or contraction of business activity which occurs over 50 or 100 years.

9. "Stagflation" refers to

(A) a simultaneous increase in output and the price level.

(B) a simultaneous reduction in output and the price level.

(C) an increase in the price level accompanied by decreases in real output and employment.

(D) a decline in the price level accompanied by increases in real output and employment.

10. Inflation is undesirable because

(A) it arbitrarily redistributes real income and wealth.

(B) it tends to be cumulative; that is, creeping inflation invariably causes hyperinflation.

(C)   it always tends to make the distribution of income less equal.

(D)   it is typically accompanied by a declining real output.

ANSWER KEY

1.	(D)		6.	(D)
2.	(B)		7.	(C)
3.	(C)		8.	(D)
4.	(A)		9.	(C)
5.	(A)		10.	(A)

CHAPTER 9

Macroeconomic Models

9.1 What a Good Macroeconomic Model Should Be Able to Do

A macroeconomic model is an abstract replica of the economy as a whole. A good model needs to be able to explain many phenomena, but there are four of particular importance.

1. Business cycles

2. Prolonged periods of high unemployment

3. Prolonged periods of high inflation

4. Simultaneous high inflation and unemployment (stagflation)

9.2 The Classical Model

The classical model is of old vintage. Aspects of the model form the basis of the beliefs of virtually all economic conservatives.

Say's Law—Named for French economist J. B. Say, the law is frequently expressed as "Supply creates its own demand." What it means is that the process of production generates enough income to buy all the product produced, and, further, there will always be enough spending to buy all the product produced. In other words, a general glut will never occur.

Using the circular flow diagram shown in Figure 9.1 for a simple pure market economy, assume that business produces $5 trillion in goods and services. This means that $5 trillion in incomes (wages, rents, interest, and profits) have been earned by households. Households will spend a portion of that, but will save also. For Say's law to work, business must borrow and use for investment spending the entire amount saved.

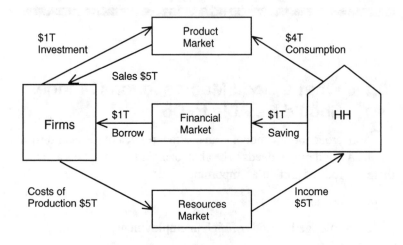

Figure 9.1 Circular Flow of Money
(Circular Flow of Goods and Services Not Shown)

Flexible Interest Rates—Flexible interest rates imply that the level of investment will always equal the level of saving. According to the classical economists, the interest rate plays a major role in explaining the levels of both saving and investment. If there is a shortage or surplus of saving, interest rates will adjust to bring saving into equality with investment. Consequently, total spending will always be just adequate to buy all the goods and services produced.

Flexible Wages and Prices—Prolonged unemployment cannot occur as long as wages are flexible. If there are unemployed workers, this must mean that wages are higher than the equilibrium. A drop in wages is all that is needed to bring the economy back to full employment.

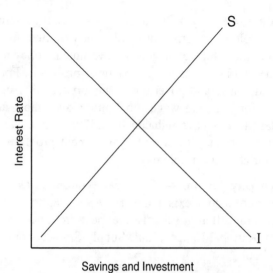

Savings and Investment

Figure 9.2 The Loanable Funds Market

While a general glut of goods and services will not occur, there can be shortages and surpluses of specific goods and services. Movements in their prices should be adequate to take care of those problems.

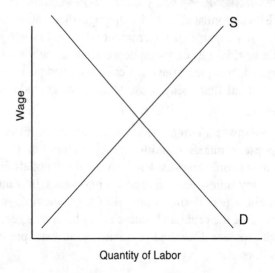

Quantity of Labor

Figure 9.3 The Labor Market

Government Policy—Given the self-regulating nature of the economy, the role of government is inherently limited. In fact, many classical economists blame misguided government policy for many of the more spectacular instances of economic problems. For example, minimum wage laws and government support for labor unions have been blamed for reducing wage flexibility. Government attempts to manage interest rates have reduced flexibility here. Government attempts to create money to pay for government programs are often blamed for inflationary problems.

Modern-Day Variants—Classical economics as a school of thought cannot be said to exist today. However, classical ideas are promoted by several different schools, the most prominent of which are Monetarism, Rational Expectations, Supply-Side economics, and the Austrian School.

9.3 The Keynesian Model (Income-Expenditure Model)

John Maynard Keynes and *The General Theory of Employment, Interest and Money* (1936)—Keynes (1883-1946, rhymes with "rains") was a British economist who had a distinguished career as a college professor, civil servant, and government advisor. In 1936, during the midst of the worldwide economic depression, he published *The General Theory* as a critique of the classical model and policies. His work was so influential that today most economists consider themselves "Keynesians."

Rigid Downward Wages—Keynes argued that while wages might rise in response to market conditions, they seldom fall. Consequently, unemployment should be considered a normal state of affairs in a capitalistic economy, unless economic policy intervenes. In addition, a general decline in wages during a period of high unemployment would probably not cure the problem because it would mean a general decline in purchasing power. Classical reasoning is an example of a fallacy of composition.

Fallacy of Composition—A fallacy of composition is when you falsely assume what is true for a part is also true for the whole. For example, if you want to see better at a football game you could stand up, but everyone could not see better if everyone stood up.

Instability of Private Investment—Contrary to classical belief, the rate of interest is not a strong determinant of either saving or investment. Saving is more influenced by income and family circumstances. Investment is more influenced by future profit expectations. Consequently, changes in the interest rate cannot be expected to equilibrate saving and investment. In fact, the two magnitudes will seldom be equal because different groups of people make the decisions and there is nothing to coordinate their decisions. In the case of investment, since it is so dependent on future expectations and since expectations are very uncertain and guided by what Keynes called "animal spirits," the level of spending is likely to be highly volatile. Instability will be the hallmark of a capitalistic economy in the absence of appropriate policy.

Paradox of Thrift—To classicals, thriftiness was unambiguously a good thing. Greater saving would automatically lead to greater investment and faster economic growth. To Keynes, greater saving was not always a good thing because there was no guarantee the saving would be converted to investment. If not, the saving would mean less spending which would lead to a contraction of production and unemployment. Thus, the paradox was that if everyone tried to save more, they might end up saving less if the economy contracted and incomes fell. This is another example of a fallacy of composition.

Fiscal Policy—Since there was no guarantee that the level of spending would equal the level of production, a role for fiscal policy was created. If government suspects too little spending will be forthcoming, it could increase its own spending or reduce taxes so that the private sector can spend more. If it suspects there will be too much spending, it can do just the opposite with its policy. Thus, government's close attention is required if we are to avoid economic instability.

It is accurate to say that Keynes provided a rationale for large-scale government participation in the economy.

Problem Solving Examples:

 What change did Keynes make in classical growth theory? How would this change affect the predictions of growth theory?

A Keynes objected to the assertion in classical growth theory that the amount of savings is determined by the interest rate. Keynes held that the amount of savings is determined by the level of income, not by the interest rate. So, a rich person will save more than a poor person, and a rich country will save more than a poor country. A poor country, with a small national income, will save little, if at all. So, there will be little capital accumulation and little growth. In contrast to this, a rich country will save more and grow faster.

By postulating a different determinant of saving (income instead of interest rates), Keynes completely altered the predictions of the classical model. Instead of poor countries growing more rapidly than rich countries, rich countries, according to Keynes, gain an even bigger advantage over poorer countries. Poor countries remain in the poverty cycle of low income, low savings, and hence low growth.

The change made by Keynes generated drastically different predictions about the relative growth rates of rich and poor countries.

Q Classical and neoclassical (marginalist) theorists have usually supported the market system of allocation. Because of this, they usually opposed government intervention in the economy. Keynes advocated government intervention. Does this mean he was against the market economy?

A If Keynes had been against the free market system, he would have advocated replacing the system. But his theory aimed to stabilize the market economy. Because of the variability of business investment, he believed that a completely free private enterprise economy was inherently unstable. So, he wanted government intervention to smooth out the fluctuations of the free enterprise economy. In his *General Theory*, he remarked that he did not care whether governments expanded their responsibilities or not; all he wanted was some government action (fiscal and monetary policy) to control inflation and unemployment.

Quiz: Macroeconomic Models

1. A macroeconomic model is a representation of

    (A) a single industry.

    (B) multiple firms.

    (C) the economy as a whole.

    (D) government actions.

2. Say's law maintains that

    (A) demand creates its own supply.

    (B) consumption creates its own demand.

    (C) savings creates its own consumption.

    (D) savings creates its own investment.

3. Classical theory states that prolonged unemployment cannot occur as long as wages are

    (A) increased.

    (B) decreased.

    (C) flexible.

    (D) held constant.

4. Classical theory ideally sees the role of government regarding the economy to be

    (A) nonexistent.

    (B) limited.

    (C)   quite active.

    (D)   demanding.

5.   In a capitalistic economy, Keynes viewed unemployment as

    (A)   unusual.

    (B)   nonexistent.

    (C)   a normal occurrence.

    (D)   catastrophic.

6.   Keynes held that the rate of interest's effect on saving or investment is

    (A)   strong.

    (B)   not a strong determinant.

    (C)   an inverse relationship.

    (D)   None of the above.

7.   Keynes' view of greater savings was that this

    (A)   was necessary to move the economy ahead.

    (B)   was not always a good thing.

    (C)   would prove disastrous.

    (D)   None of the above.

8.   Keynes held that government's fiscal policy role in the economy should be

    (A)   significant.

    (B)   nonexistent.

    (C)   minimal at best.

    (D)   None of the above.

9. Keynes suggested that for the capitalist economy to survive, it has to

    (A) include elements of socialism.

    (B) grow.

    (C) periodically contract.

    (D) keep the government's budget balanced.

10. Keynes' writings

    (A) support Say's law.

    (B) dispute Say's law.

    (C) are not related to the subject of Say's law.

    (D) are practically in agreement with Say's law.

ANSWER KEY

1.	(C)	6.	(B)
2.	(D)	7.	(B)
3.	(C)	8.	(A)
4.	(D)	9.	(B)
5.	(C)	10.	(B)

CHAPTER 10

The Income-
Expenditure Model

Turning Say's Law on its head, the simple income-expenditure model essentially incorporates the idea that "demand creates its own supply." Consequently, the level of spending, or aggregate expenditure (AE), is a major focus. Much of the analysis is directed toward analyzing the levels of the various types of spending:

$$AE = C + I + G + (X - M)$$

where C is consumption, I is investment, G is government spending, and $(X - M)$ is net exports (X is exports and M is imports).

10.1 Consumption Spending

Household Consumption Schedule—The household consumption schedule shows the relationship between a household's disposable income and its consumption spending. Increases in a household's disposable income should cause increases in its consumption spending.

Household Savings Schedule—The household savings schedule shows the relationship between a household's disposable income and its savings. Increases in a household's disposable income should cause increases in its savings.

Break-even Level—All income is consumed at the break-even level. There is no savings. At levels of income lower than break-even, the household is dissaving. Households can do this over short periods of times by drawing down on assets.

Average Propensity to Consume (APC)—The proportion of income consumed.

$$APC = C/DI$$

Average Propensity to Save (APS)—The proportion of income saved.

$$APS = S/DI$$

$$APC + APS = 1$$

The proportion of income consumed plus the proportion saved must equal 100%.

Marginal Propensity to Consume (MPC)—The proportion of additional income consumed.

$$MPC = \Delta C/\Delta DI$$

Marginal Propensity to Save (MPS)—The proportion of additional income saved.

$$MPS = \Delta S/\Delta DI$$

$$MPC + MPS = 1$$

The proportion of additional income consumed plus the proportion saved must equal 100%.

DI	C	S	APC	APS	MPC	MPS
10000	12000	−2000	1.20	−0.20	–	–
12000	13500	−1500	1.13	−0.13	0.75	0.25
14000	15000	−1000	1.07	−0.07	0.75	0.25
16000	16500	−500	1.03	−0.03	0.75	0.25
18000	18000	0	1.00	0.00	0.75	0.25
20000	19500	500	0.98	0.03	0.75	0.25
22000	21000	1000	0.95	0.05	0.75	0.25
24000	22500	1500	0.94	0.06	0.75	0.25
26000	24000	2000	0.92	0.08	0.75	0.25
28000	25500	2500	0.91	0.09	0.75	0.25

Table 10.1 Household Consumption and Savings Schedules

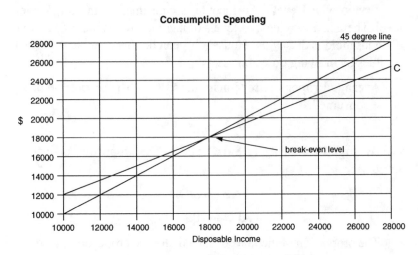

Figure 10.1 Household Consumption Schedule

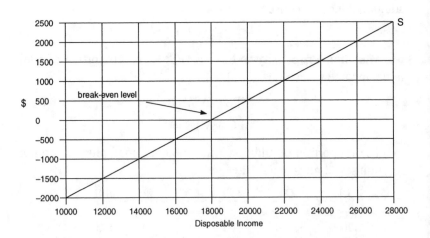

Figure 10.2 Household Savings Schedule

---

45 degree line

A 45 degree line bisects a graph quadrant forming an angle of 45 degrees with both the horizontal and vertical axes. Any point on a 45 degree line represents equal horizontal and vertical distances. Forty-five degree lines are included in many graphs used in economics because they make reading the graph easier.

Shifts in the household consumption and savings schedules — The schedules will shift due to changes in household thriftiness, number of members in the household, changes in the age of household members, and the household's wealth. An upward (downward) shift in the consumption (savings) schedule means the household wants to consume more out of its disposable income.

National Consumption Schedule—The national consumption schedule shows the relationship between the national level of disposable income and the national level of consumption. Note the similarity between the national and household schedules.

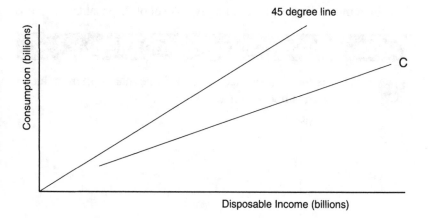

Figure 10.3 National Consumption Schedule

National Savings Schedule—The national savings schedule shows the relationship between the national level of disposable income and the national level of savings. Note the similarity between the national and household schedules.

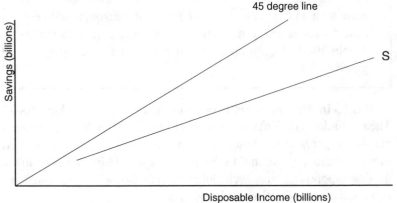

Figure 10.4 National Savings Schedule

Shifts in the national consumption and savings schedules—The schedules will shift due to changes in national thriftiness, interest rates, the price level, and national wealth. An upward (downward) shift in the consumption (savings) schedule indicates that consumers wish to consume more (save less) out of a given level of disposable income.

Problem Solving Examples:

 What is the significance of the 45° line that is often included in the consumption function diagram?

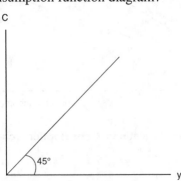

A The 45° line, as shown in the figure, traces out the only points in the entire diagram where the quantity being measured on the vertical axis is exactly equal to the quantity being measured on the horizontal axis. In the consumption function diagram, consumption is measured on the vertical axis and income is measured on the horizontal axis. Here, the significance of the 45° line is that it indicates the points where consumption is exactly equal to income. Wherever a given consumption function crosses this line, income is equal to consumption at this income level, and so saving is equal to zero.

Q

Disposable income after taxes	Net Savings
$8,000	100
$9,000	250

What is the marginal propensity to consume in the range $8,000–$9,000 for the family given in the figure?

A Two definitions are needed to solve this problem. First, the marginal propensity to consume = the change in consumption/ the change in income. Second, recall that

Consumption + Savings = Disposable Income

or,

Consumption = Disposable Income – Savings.

In the example above, income increased by $9,000 – $8,000 = $1,000. Savings increased by $250 – $100 = $150. Therefore, consumption increased by $1,000 – $150 = $850.

$$\text{Then MPC} = 850/1000$$
$$= 0.85$$

10.2 Investment

Rate of return on investment—The rate of return is a measure of the profitability of an investment. It compares the profits earned on an investment with the size of the initial investment. Rate of return formulas are complicated in most realistic cases. For an investment that will last forever and return the same profit every year, the formula is:

rate of return = (annual profit)/(investment)

For example, if a $10 million factory will earn a profit of $1 million a year forever, then the rate of return is $1 million/$10 million = 10%.

Marginal Efficiency of Investment (MEI)—The marginal efficiency of investment schedule shows the rate of return on the last dollar invested.

Firm's MEI Schedule—Projects A through E are ranked by (expected) rate of return. The width of each rectangle indicates the amount of investment required for each. The interest rate (measuring the opportunity cost of funds to the firm) is represented by the horizontal line. The firm will invest in every project that promises to pay a rate of return in excess of the interest rate, in this case projects A, B, and C. Were the interest rate to fall (downward shift in interest rate line), more projects might become worthwhile. If the interest rate rises, the firm might invest in fewer projects.

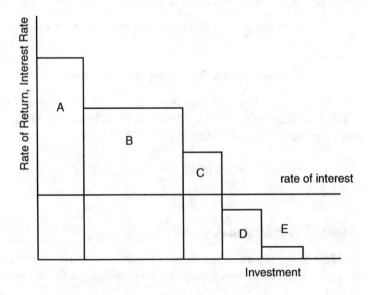

Figure 10.5 Firm's MEI Schedule

Economy's MEI Schedule—For the economy as a whole, there are so many projects that the MEI schedule becomes a smooth curve. The economy's level of investment is determined by the intersection of the MEI schedule and the rate of interest. Increases in the rate of interest will reduce investment spending; decreases will raise investment spending.

Shifts in the MEI schedule—The MEI schedule will shift as a result in changes in:

1. expected product demand

2. technology and innovation

3. cost of new capital goods

4. corporate income tax rates

Factors causing firms to want to invest more at any interest rate will shift the MEI curve outward/upward/rightward. Factors causing firms to want to invest less at any interest rate will shift the MEI curve inward/downward/leftward.

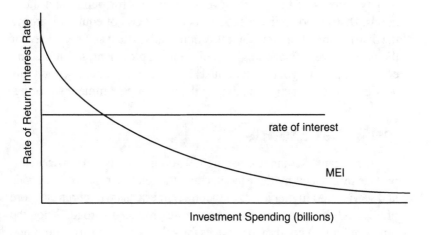

Figure 10.6 Economy's MEI Schedule

Problem Solving Example:

There are many factors which affect the amount of investment undertaken at any given time. List six important factors.

The six main "non-interest" determinants of investment are:

1) acquisition, maintenance, and operating costs to the producer;

2) business taxes;

3) technological change;

4) the stock of capital goods on hand;

5) expectations about future sales and future profitability; and

6) the rate of interest.

10.3 Government Spending

The level of government spending is determined by allocational, distributional, and stabilization needs. Allocational needs reflect society's views of the proper level of spending for public and merit goods. Distributional needs reflect society's views of equity regarding the distribution of income. Stabilization needs reflect society's view of the proper level of spending to achieve unemployment, inflation, and economic growth goals. Economists have not gone much beyond this very general statement in analyzing the level of government spending.

10.4 Net Exports

Americans' willingness to purchase foreign goods and services (import) is influenced by their income and the relative price of the goods and services. At higher levels of income, Americans will purchase more of all goods and services, including those produced abroad. When the prices of foreign goods and services fall relative to domestic goods and services, more foreign goods and services will be demanded.

Foreign export demand is similarly determined.

10.5 Equilibrium in a Closed Private Economy

Assumptions of the model—A closed, private economy is one with no international trade and no government. Hence, the expression for Aggregate Expenditure is that shown in the box. The level of investment is autonomous. The price level is fixed.

$$AE = C + I$$

Autonomous Spending—Spending is autonomous if its level is not influenced by the level of income. It may be influenced by other factors.

Induced Spending—Spending is induced if its level is influenced by the level of income.

Inventory Change—In the simple model, inventory change refers to unexpected increases or decreases in firms' inventory holdings. This happens when firms incorrectly anticipate what the market will be willing to buy.

THREE WAYS TO IDENTIFY EQUILIBRIUM:

1. AE equal to GNP indicates a point of equilibrium. If AE > GNP, then current production is insufficient to satisfy demand. Firms may be forced to draw down on their inventories. Firms will respond to this situation by hiring more resources and expanding production. If AE < GNP, firms cannot sell all their current production. Unsold goods will be placed in inventory causing firms to reduce production in layoff resources. If AE = GNP, then current production is just adequate to satisfy demand. There is no reason to expand or reduce production so there is equilibrium.

2. S = I indicates a point of equilibrium. If I > S then current production is insufficient to satisfy demand, and the economy will expand. If I < S, then current production exceeds demand, and the economy will contract.

3. Equilibrium is also found where inventory change is 0. If inventory change is negative, current production was inadequate to meet

demand so inventories were drawn down leading firms to expand production to satisfy demand and rebuild inventories. If inventory change is positive, current production exceeded demand and the excess was placed in inventory leading firms to reduce production.

GNP	C	S	I	AE	Inventory Change	Condition of Economy
3500	3125	375	500	3625	-125	expand
3600	3200	400	500	3700	-100	expand
3700	3275	425	500	3775	-75	expand
3800	3350	450	500	3850	-50	expand
3900	3425	475	500	3925	-25	expand
4000	3500	500	500	4000	0	equilibrium
4100	3575	525	500	4075	25	contract
4200	3650	550	500	4150	50	contract
4300	3725	575	500	4225	75	contract
4400	3800	600	500	4300	100	contract

Table 10.2 Equilibrium in a Closed, Private Economy

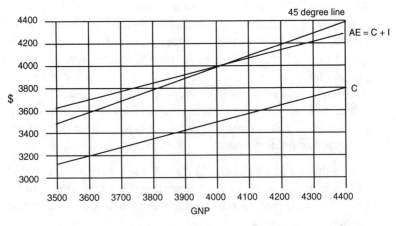

Figure 10.7 Equilibrium in a Closed, Private Economy

Problem Solving Examples:

Q Give the significance of the equilibrium level of output.

A The equilibrium level of output is that level of output which the economy is capable and willing to sustain. Stated differently, the equilibrium level of output whose production will actually create total spending just sufficient to purchase that output; in other words, the total quantity of goods supplied (NNP) is precisely equal to the total quantity of goods demanded (C + In). This is the only level of output at which the economy is willing to spend precisely the amount necessary to take that output off the market. Here, the annual rates of production and spending are in balance. There is no over production, which results in a piling up of unsold goods and therefore, cutbacks in the rate of production, nor is there an excess of total spending, which "draws" down inventories and prompts increases in the rate of production.

Q Assuming that equilibrium GNP can be found at the intersection of the savings and investment schedules, show that equilibrium GNP can be found at the intersection of the consumption plus investment schedule and the 45° line.

A Look at the graph on the following page to help visualize the problem. Aggregate demand equals consumption plus investment.

$$Y_d = C + I \qquad (1)$$

Aggregate supply = aggregate income which equals the sum of consumption and savings

$$Y_s = C + S \qquad (2)$$

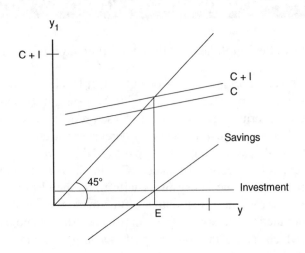

In equilibrium, aggregate demand equals aggregate supply

$$Y_d = Y_s \qquad\qquad (3)$$

i.e., the intersection of the consumption-investment schedules and the 45° line. Substituting (1) and (2) into (3) results in

$$C + I = C + S$$

Suppressing consumption at both sides of the equation gives

$$I = S$$

i.e., the intersection of the investment and savings schedules.

10.6 The Multiplier

The Multiplier Principle—Increases in autonomous spending will cause GNP to increase by a multiple of the initial increase in spending. Intuitively, suppose business increases its spending for investment goods. This will increase incomes in the investment goods industries by an equivalent amount. Out of this new income, the employees and owners of the investment goods industries will be able to increase their own consumption. This spending raises income in the consumption goods industries. The owners and employees of the consumptions goods industries will then be able to increase their spending which will raise income and spending elsewhere in the economy. In short, additional spending raises incomes which leads to additional spending which raises incomes still more which leads to further spending which raises incomes, and so on.

Investment multiplier—The investment multiplier measures how much GNP will be created by an additional dollar of autonomous investment. In the example (Table 10.3 and Figure 10.10), an increase in investment of 25 caused the equilibrium level of GNP to rise by 100. Therefore, the investment multiplier was ΔGNP/ ΔI = 4. In a simple income-expenditure model the formula for the investment multiplier is $1/(1 - MPC)$. To compute the effect of additional investment on GNP use the following formula:

$$\Delta I \times 1/(1 - MPC) = \Delta GNP$$

Figure 10.8 The Investment Multiplier

Consumption multiplier—The consumption multiplier measures how much GNP will be created by an additional dollar of autonomous consumption. In the example (Table 10.4 and Figure 10.9), an increase in autonomous consumption of 25 caused the equilibrium level of GNP to rise by 100. Therefore, the consumption multiplier is ΔGNP/ΔC = 4.

GNP	C	S	I	I´	AE	AE´	Inventory Change	Inventory Change´
3500	3125	375	500	525	3625	3650	–125	–150
3600	3200	400	500	525	3700	3725	–100	–125
3700	3275	425	500	525	3775	3800	–75	–100
3800	3350	450	500	525	3850	3875	–50	–75
3900	3425	475	500	525	3925	3950	–25	–50
4000	3500	500	500	525	4000	4025	0	–25
4100	3575	525	500	525	4075	4100	25	0
4200	3650	550	500	525	4150	4175	50	25
4300	3725	575	500	525	4225	4250	75	50
4400	3800	600	500	525	4300	4325	100	75

Table 10.3 Investment Multiplier

In a simple income-expenditure model the formula for the consumption multiplier is $1/(1 - \text{MPC})$. To compute the effect of additional consumption on GNP use the following formula:

$$\Delta C \times 1/(1 - \text{MPC}) = \Delta \text{GNP}$$

GNP	C	S	C´	S´	I	AE	AE´	Inventory Change	Inventory Change´
3500	3125	375	3150	350	500	3625	3650	–125	–150
3600	3200	400	3225	375	500	3700	3725	–100	–125
3700	3275	425	3300	400	500	3775	3800	–75	–100
3800	3350	450	3375	425	500	3850	3875	–50	–75
3900	3425	475	3450	450	500	3925	3950	–25	–50
4000	3500	500	3525	475	500	4000	4025	0	–25
4100	3575	525	3600	500	500	4075	4100	25	0
4200	3650	550	3675	525	500	4150	4175	50	25
4300	3725	575	3750	550	500	4225	4250	75	50
4400	3800	600	3825	575	500	4300	4325	100	75

Table 10.4 Consumption Multiplier

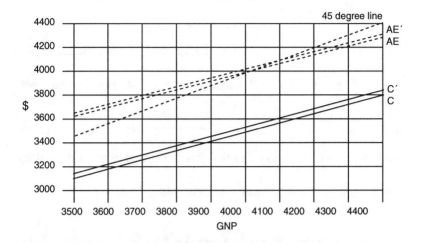

Figure 10.9 The Consumption Multiplier

Problem Solving Example:

Prove that the multiplier is equal to 1/(1 – MPC).

Suppose you purchase an item for $100. This first $100 will result in an increase in income throughout the economy. The $100 will find its way into the hands of other households in the form of wages, rent, interest, and profits. There it will be subject to MPC. Suppose MPC = 0.8. Then (100) (0.8) = $80 will be spent. This $80 will contribute to income and will once again pass on to other households. There it will once again be subject to MPC. So (80)(0.8) [= (100)(0.8)²] = $64 will be spent. The process will keep going.

Generalizing, we see that if x is the original expenditure and c is MPC, the amount of eventual income, I, can be determined by this formula:

$$I = x + xc + xc^2 + xc^3 + \dots$$
$$= x(1 + c + c^2 + c^3 + \dots)$$

This is an infinite series with c smaller than one; therefore,

$\left(1 + c + c^2 + c^3 + K = \dfrac{1}{1-c}\right)$. Substituting back into the original equa-

tion, we get $I = x\left(\dfrac{1}{1-c}\right)$ or $1 = x\left(\dfrac{1}{1-\text{MPC}}\right)$. So we see that the In-

come generated, I, is equal to the original investment multiplied by

$\left(\dfrac{1}{1-\text{MPC}}\right)$, which is therefore the multiplier.

10.7 Macroeconomic Problems

Potential GNP—Potential GNP is the amount of output the economy is capable of producing at full employment. In the Keynesian model, there is nothing automatically pushing the economy toward potential GNP.

Recessionary Gap—Insufficient spending will lead the economy to an equilibrium below potential GNP. The recessionary gap measures the shortfall in aggregate expenditure. In Figure 10.10, potential GNP = 4100. The level of spending is AE. AE´ is the level needed to achieve potential. The gap is the vertical distance between AE and AE´ at potential GNP. The gap represents the Keynesian idea that recessions are caused by too little spending, and that more spending is the solution.

Inflationary Gap—Too much spending will lead the economy to an equilibrium above potential GNP. Since the economy is not capable of producing more than its potential for extended periods of time, what must happen is that the average price level must rise. The inflationary gap measures the excess in aggregate expenditure. In Figure 10.11, potential GNP = 3900. AE is the level of spending. Note AE exceeds GNP at potential. AE´ is the level of spending that would not put upward pressure on prices. The gap is the vertical distance between AE and AE´ at potential GNP. The gap represents the Keynesian idea that inflation is caused by too much spending, and that reducing spending is the solution.

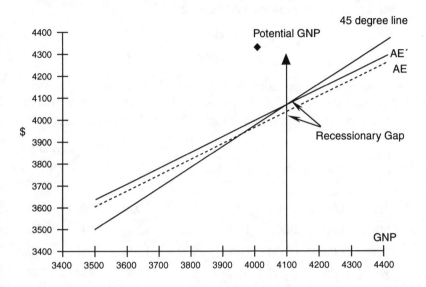

Figure 10.10 Recessionary Gap

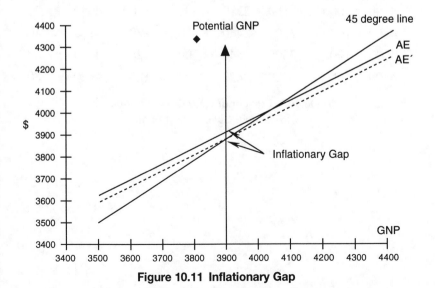

Figure 10.11 Inflationary Gap

10.8 Fiscal Policy

Fiscal policy-Equilibrium in a model with a government sector—When government is allowed in the model:

$$AE = C + I + G$$

$$DI = GNP - T$$

Taxes are a complicating factor because they can affect both households and firms. In the simplest model, the assumption made is that taxes are of the lump-sum variety and are levied only on households.

GNP	T	DI	C	I	G	AE	Inventory Change
3500	1000	2500	1900	500	1200	3600	−100
3600	1000	2600	1980	500	1200	3680	−80
3700	1000	2700	2060	500	1200	3760	−60
3800	1000	2800	2140	500	1200	3840	−40
3900	1000	2900	2220	500	1200	3920	−20
4000	1000	3000	2300	500	1200	4000	0
4100	1000	3100	2380	500	1200	4080	20
4200	1000	3200	2460	500	1200	4160	40
4300	1000	3300	2540	500	1200	4240	60
4400	1000	3400	2620	500	1200	4320	80

**Table 10.5 Equilibrium in a Closed Economy
with Simple Government Sector**

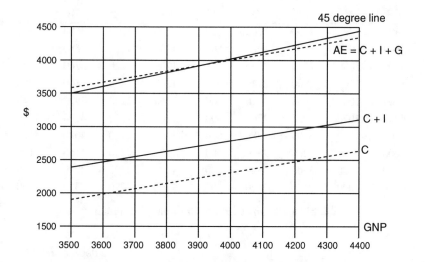

**Figure 10.12 Equilibrium in a Closed Economy with
Simple Government Sector**

THREE WAYS TO FIND EQUILIBRIUM:

Like the simpler model, there are three ways to find equilibrium.
The conditions AE = GNP and Inventory change = 0 are unchanged.
The S = I condition is replaced by the slightly more complicated

$$S + T = I + G$$

Government Spending Multiplier—The government spending
multiplier measures how much GNP will be created by a dollar of government spending. In the example (Table 10.6 and Figure 10.13), an
increase in G of 20 causes GNP to rise by 100. The government spending multiplier is ΔGNP/ΔG = 5. The formula is government spending
multiplier = 1/(1 – MPC), where the MPC is calculated as C/GNP. To
compute the impact of government spending on GNP use:

$$\Delta G \times 1/(1 - MPC) = GNP$$

GNP	T	DI	C	I	G	G´	AE	AE´
3500	1000	2500	1900	500	1200	1220	3600	3620
3600	1000	2600	1980	500	1200	1220	3680	3700
3700	1000	2700	2060	500	1200	1220	3760	3780
3800	1000	2800	2140	500	1200	1220	3840	3860
3900	1000	2900	2220	500	1200	1220	3920	3940
4000	1000	3000	2300	500	1200	1220	4000	4020
4100	1000	3100	2380	500	1200	1220	4080	4100
4200	1000	3200	2460	500	1200	1220	4160	4180
4300	1000	3300	2540	500	1200	1220	4240	4260
4400	1000	3400	2620	500	1200	1220	4320	4340

Table 10.6 Government Spending Multiplier

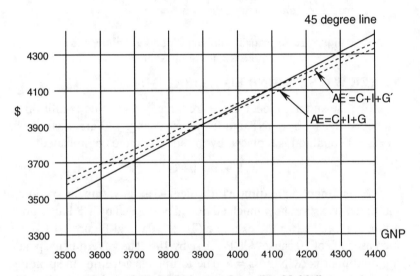

Figure 10.13 Government Spending Multiplier

Tax Multiplier—The tax multiplier measures how much GNP will be reduced by a dollar in additional taxes. Intuitively, when taxes are raised, consumer disposable income is reduced. This will reduce consumption spending leading to a multiplied decrease in GNP. In the example (Table 10.7 and Figure 10.14), an increase in T of 25 will reduce C by 20 (ΔT $\times$ MPC), where the MPC is defined as ΔC/ΔDI. The reduced C will cause GNP to fall by 100. The tax multiplier is ΔGNP/ΔT

= –4. The formula for the tax multiplier is –MPC/(1 – MPC), where the MPC is defined as $\Delta C/\Delta GNP$. To compute the impact of tax increases on GNP, use:

$$\Delta T \times -MPC/(1 - MPC) = \Delta GNP$$

Balanced Budget Multiplier—The balanced budget multiplier measures how much GNP will be created by a dollar increase in both G and T (maintaining the current budget balance). Intuitively, the increase in G will raise GNP by a multiple amount. The increase in T will reduce GNP by a multiple amount, but the net effect will be positive because government spending has a stronger stimulative effect than taxes have dampening effect. This is because tax changes do not translate dollar for dollar into consumption cuts. Saving absorbs some of the change. From the chart (Table 10.8), an increase in G and T of 100 will cause GNP to increase by 100. The balanced budget multiplier is equal to 1. To compute the impact of a balanced budget increase on GNP use:

$$\Delta B \times 1 = \Delta GNP, \text{ where } \Delta B = \Delta G = \Delta T$$

GNP	T	T´	DI	DI´	C	C´	I	G	AE	AE´
3500	1000	1025	2500	2475	1900	1880	500	1200	3600	3580
3600	1000	1025	2600	2575	1980	1960	500	1200	3680	3660
3700	1000	1025	2700˙	2675	2060	2040	500	1200	3760	3740
3800	1000	1025	2800	2775	2140	2120	500	1200	3840	3820
3900	1000	1025	2900	2875	2220	2200	500	1200	3920	3900
4000	1000	1025	3000	2975	2300	2280	500	1200	4000	3980
4100	1000	1025	3100	3075	2380	2360	500	1200	4080	4060
4200	1000	1025	3200	3175	2460	2440	500	1200	4160	4140
4300	1000	1025	3300	3275	2540	2520	500	1200	4240	4220
4400	1000	1025	3400	3375	2620	2600	500	1200	4320	4300

Table 10.7 Tax Multiplier

GNP	T	T´	DI	DI´	C	C´	I	G	G´	AE	AE´
3500	1000	1100	2500	2400	1900	1820	500	1200	1300	3600	3620
3600	1000	1100	2600	2500	1980	1900	500	1200	1300	3680	3700
3700	1000	1100	2700	2600	2060	1980	500	1200	1300	3760	3780
3800	1000	1100	2800	2700	2140	2060	500	1200	1300	3840	3860
3900	1000	1100	2900	2800	2220	2140	500	1200	1300	3920	3940
4000	1000	1100	3000	2900	2300	2220	500	1200	1300	4000	4020
4100	1000	1100	3100	3000	2380	2300	500	1200	1300	4080	4100
4200	1000	1100	3200	3100	2460	2380	500	1200	1300	4160	4180
4300	1000	1100	3300	3200	2540	2460	500	1200	1300	4240	4260
4400	1000	1100	3400	3300	2620	2540	500	1200	1300	4320	4340

Table 10.8 Balanced Budget Multiplier

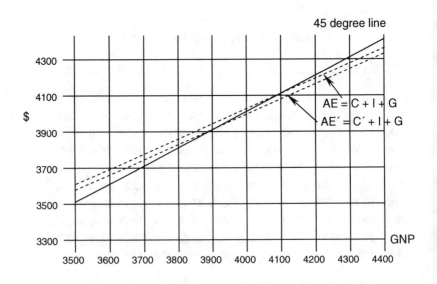

Figure 10.14 Tax Multiplier

Quiz: The Income-Expenditure Model

1. At the break even point

    (A) saving is equal to zero.

    (B) consumption is equal to disposable income.

    (C) MPS + MPC = 1.

    (D) All of the above.

2. The marginal propensity to consume is the ratio of

    (A) total consumption to total income.

    (B) the increase in saving to an increase in income.

    (C) the increase in consumption to an increase in income.

    (D) the increase in consumption to an increase in saving.

3. The level of consumer income determines

    (A) the stock of liquid assets.

    (B) the level of consumer indebtedness.

    (C) the purchasing power.

    (D) the distribution of wealth.

4. If MPS is .25, then MPC is

    (A) .25.

    (B) $.25 \times .75$.

(C) .25 – 1.0.

(D) 1.0 – .25.

5. On a chart which shows consumption and income, a 45° line shows

(A) the set of all points where consumption equals saving.

(B) the set of all points where saving equals income.

(C) the set of all points where consumption equals income.

(D) all by itself, the level of saving for all income levels.

6. Which of the following would tend to shift the investment schedule downward?

(A) An increase in the interest rate

(B) A technological advance which causes costs to decrease sharply

(C) Vigorous stock market activity on Wall Street

(D) Declining wages

7. The values of MPC and MPS always add up to 1 because

(A) any two marginal quantities add up to 1.

(B) both MPC and MPS schedules are straight lines.

(C) every $1 of the national income is either saved or used for consumption.

(D) the level of investment in the economy is assumed to be constant.

8. The equilibrium point at which I = S makes an economy stable due to the fact that

    (A) anywhere away from this point the economy is naturally driven towards the equilibrium.

    (B) people want to use their resources productively and therefore reinvest all that they save.

    (C) government stops intervening at this point.

    (D) All of the above.

9. If a multiplier is 1 then

    (A) consumers save all of their income.

    (B) there is no multiplier effect.

    (C) the aggregate demand is practically nonexistent.

    (D) All of the above.

10. The recessionary gap is likely to have a stronger impact on the economy when

    (A) MPS is small.

    (B) MPC is small.

    (C) MPS is large.

    (D) Both (B) and (C).

ANSWER KEY

1.	(D)	6.	(A)
2.	(C)	7.	(C)
3.	(C)	8.	(A)
4.	(D)	9.	(D)
5.	(C)	10.	(A)

CHAPTER 11

Fiscal Policy Issues

11.1 Stabilization Policy

Discretionary Fiscal Policy—Discretionary fiscal policy refers to changes in government spending and taxes consciously made by the government to achieve certain stabilization goals. For example, if the economy threatens to head into a recession, and the government makes a decision to cut taxes to maintain purchasing power, that is a discretionary action.

Automatic Stabilizers—The level of spending of some government programs is automatically influenced by the state of the economy. For example, when unemployment goes up, government spending for unemployment compensation automatically increases. In a similar manner, the revenue received from most forms of taxes is also influenced by the economy. For example, personal income tax collections fall during recessions as wages drop and people lose their jobs. Thus, during recessions, government spending automatically rises and tax collections fall. During periods of full or near-full employment (when inflation dangers are greatest), automatically, government spending falls and tax collections rise. Both sets of actions are what the theory of fiscal policy would call for in those situations. These economy-sensitive programs are called automatic stabilizers because they automatically work to stabilize the economy. As a general rule, automatic stabilizers cannot cure recessions or inflation, but make the problem less severe than it otherwise would be.

The Budget Cycle—During the period January through September, the president proposes a budget and Congress accepts, amends, or rejects the proposals. The budget decided upon goes into effect on October 1 and remains in effect through the following September 30, a period known as the fiscal year. The budget process is a lengthy one, and deciding on a proper budget to meet the stabilization needs of the economy requires the ability to forecast accurately more than one year into the future, something economists are not good at. Many economists believe these considerations vitiate the effectiveness of fiscal policy as a stabilization tool.

Full Employment or Structural Budget—The full employment budget is an estimate of what government spending, taxes, and the deficit would be if the economy were at full employment. Its purpose is to get a better picture of how expansionary or contractionary the government's budget is. The problem with using actual spending, tax, and deficit figures is that each of these factors is influenced by the state of the economy. For example, the government may enact an austere budget (limited spending and high taxes), yet if there is a recession, automatic stabilizers may lead to greater spending, lower taxes and a larger deficit, which would be a misleading picture of what the actual budget intended. By estimating spending, taxes, and the deficit at full employment, we remove the effect of the economy on the budget.

Functional Finance—Under a system of functional finance, government spending and taxes are set to meet the stabilization needs of the economy (run deficit during recession and surplus during inflation), with little concern given to the resulting deficit and surplus.

11.2 Deficits and the Public Debt

Size of the Deficit and Public Debt—In 1988, the U.S. Government ran a deficit of approximately $155 billion, leaving the U.S. Government with a debt of approximately $2.6 trillion at the end of 1988. Both are "big" numbers, but there are some considerations that put these numbers in perspective:

1. A significant portion of the debt, approximately $550 billion, was owed to agencies of the U.S. Government (Federal Re-

serve System, Social Security Trust Fund, etc.), leaving a net debt of approximately $2.1 trillion.

2. Only 13% of this net debt was owed to foreign nations, although this percentage has been growing in recent years (see discussion of Internal Debt below).

3. The burden of debt to an entity can only be properly assessed by comparing it to the entity's financial condition. Using a household analogy, a $20,000 debt is less burdensome to a household earning $150,000 per year than one earning $20,000. In the case of deficits and the debt, a useful comparison is with GNP. Figure 11.1 compares annual deficits with GNP. Recent deficit-to-GNP ratios have been higher than average, but there have been periods in our history when they have been even higher. Figure 11.2 shows the Debt-to-GNP ratio. Although this has risen in recent years, it remains considerably below the level at the end of World War II (a war we won, while piling up huge amounts of debt). Figure 11.3 shows the ratio of interest payments on the debt to GNP, which tells a similar story to the two previous figures.

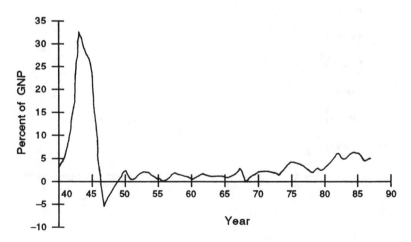

Figure 11.1 Trend in Deficit Relative to GNP

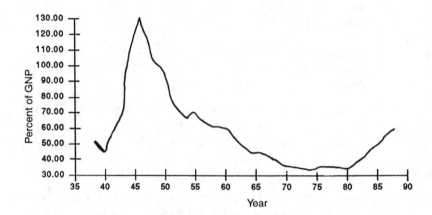

Figure 11.2 Trend in Debt Relative to GNP

Internal Debt—An internal debt is one we "owe to ourselves." If the debt issued by the government is purchased by Americans, then it is an internal debt. An internal debt is considered easier to maintain. Most of the debt of the U.S. government is an internal debt.

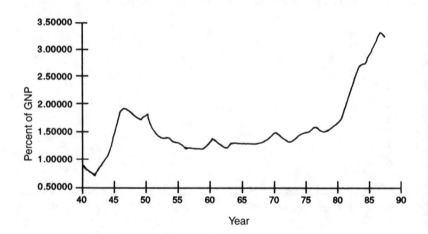

Figure 11.3 Trend in Interest Payments Relative to GNP

External Debt—An external debt is one we owe to an outside institution. External debts are considered more onerous than internal debts because to service and pay them back we must give up assets.

Refinancing the Debt—Most government (and corporate) debt is paid back by refinancing. This means that the government borrows from other sources to pay back the creditors whose loans have become due.

National Bankruptcy—Bankruptcy occurs when a unit is unable to pay its debts. This is unlikely to happen in the case of the United States. Since the debt is largely internal, we can simply tax ourselves to pay ourselves back. There may be distributional problems here. If worst came to worst, the government could simply print money.

Crowding Out—One of the generally agreed upon problems of the public debt is crowding out. This occurs when the public debt has the effect of reducing (or crowding out) private investment. At one level, we can say that the money the government borrows is no longer available to be borrowed by the private sector. At another level, government borrowing increases the demand for credit which raises interest rates. The higher interest rates crowd out private sector investment. If there is less investment, the economy will not grow as fast. Crowding out should only be a problem when the economy is at or near full employment. Also, if the government spending financed is used to produce valuable assets, the problem is reduced.

Deficits and Inflation—While budget deficits are frequently accused of being inflationary, the truth is a bit more complicated. Deficits can be inflationary, but it depends when they are incurred. Deficits occurring when the economy is at or near full employment can be inflationary because they can cause an inflationary gap situation. When the economy is operating well below potential, inflationary problems are unlikely, and deficits may be needed to get the economy moving again.

Attempts at Balanced Budget Legislation—As a result of the huge budget deficits incurred during the Reagan administration, Congress passed and the president signed the Gramm-Rudman-Hollings Balanced Budget Law in 1985. The law mandates that the government reduce the budget deficit to progressively smaller specified levels each year until the deficit is eliminated in 1991. This law ultimately collapsed and had no real meaning, as there was no mechanism in the legislation to enforce automatic spending cuts. Second, the deficit targets were considered met if they were consistent with the government's economic forecast. When the forecasts proved too optimistic, then the deficit targets were not achieved.

Even past 1991, federal budget deficits continued to swell, and interest on the national debt took over a substantial portion of the annual federal budget. Though the budget deficits in the 1990s under President Bill Clinton decreased relative to the deficits run during the administrations of Reagan and George Bush, there was still a substantial shortfall in revenues to expenditures. There was also no reasonable expectation on the part of economists or government officials of a balanced budget until well into the next century.

In reaction to the public's concern over the rising tide of debt, Congress, with strong support from the Republican majority that took power in 1994, proposed a Balanced Budget Amendment to the Constitution.

Problem Solving Examples:

Q Explain the crowding-out effect.

A The crowding-out effect of the sale of Treasury bonds is that these additional bonds take funds away from private borrowers who would otherwise contribute to aggregate demand.

When bonds are sold to the commercial banks and bank reserves, and thus the total amount of bank credit remains unchanged, commercial banks must cut down on the volume of loans made to the private sector of the economy. This reduces the private capital expenditures that might have been financed by these loans.

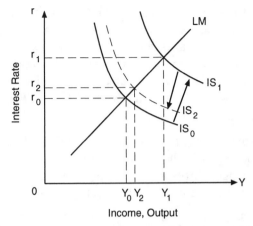

Income, Output

If there were no increase in the money supply, rates of return would have to rise in order to induce persons to hold more bonds, stocks, and physical assets relative to their money holdings. But the higher rates of return would reduce the supply of these other assets because higher rates of return are more difficult to earn. As a result, the issue of U.S. government securities would tend to be offset by a reduction in private investment. In this case, the aggregate demand would be almost unchanged (see the figure above).

The initial stimulus of the government deficit shifts the IS schedule from IS_0 to IS_1, and income and interest rate have the tendency to rise to Y_1 and r_1, respectively. But the crowding-out effect reduces private investment, the IS curve shifts back to position IS_2, and income and interest rates reach only the levels Y_2 and r_2, respectively.

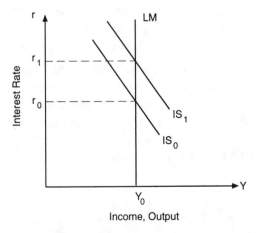

Income, Output

Monetarist economists, such as Milton Friedman, hold the view that government spending merely crowds out private spending. The crowding-out effect is also implied when it is assumed that the LM curve is vertical. This implies that the demand for money is not related to the interest rate: there is only a unique level of income at which the money market is in equilibrium (see the figure on the bottom of the previous page).

When government spending increases and the IS schedule shifts to the North-East, only the interest rate is increased, but the income remains unchanged. Investment spending is reduced by an amount exactly equal to the increase in government spending.

 Is the fact that there is a public debt of $350 billion a reason for concern? Discuss.

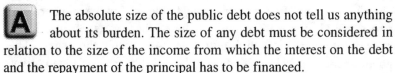 The absolute size of the public debt does not tell us anything about its burden. The size of any debt must be considered in relation to the size of the income from which the interest on the debt and the repayment of the principal has to be financed.

In 1935 the gross federal debt was only about $35 billion, one-tenth of the debt. Gross national product was $72 billion. Thus in 1935 the income/debt ratio, or debt turnover ratio, was 72/35 = 2.06. Nowadays national income is about $980 billion. Thus the income debt ratio has increased to 2.8. The present economy can better afford to carry this debt than in the 1930s. The interest paid by the federal government is about $18 billion. The whole of the American debt is held internally: the American people owe the money to themselves. Paying off the internally held debt does not therefore mean a change in the total wealth of the nation, but it will probably result in a redistribution of this wealth.

Wars have been chiefly responsible for the large size of the debt, and they imposed most of their burdens on those who were living at the time: productive factors were used for the production of military goods instead of civilian goods and services. No additional capital goods were supplied to increase the production for the succeeding generation. Not the public debt, but the real economic sacrifice, forms the real burden.

CHAPTER 12

Money And Banking

12.1 What Money Is and Does

Money—Money is anything that is **generally acceptable** in exchange for goods and services and in payment of debts. Suppose you had something you wanted to sell. Few would be willing to part with their product for a commodity like a loaf of bread, a chicken, or an automobile hubcap. All would be willing to exchange their product for coins, currency, or a check. Therefore, these latter items are money because they are generally acceptable. Everybody is willing to accept them in exchange for what they want to sell.

Functions of Money—Money performs four particular functions:

1. **Medium of Exchange**—Money is used to facilitate exchanges of goods and services. Money makes buying and selling easier. Assume we had an economy where nothing was money. Such an economy is known as a **barter economy**. In a barter economy goods and services exchange directly for other goods and services. If you want an axe that someone is selling, you must find an item that person wants to trade for it. Barter requires a **double coincidence** of wants, each party must want what the other party has. If that condition does not hold, then exchange cannot take place, and valuable resources can be wasted in putting together trades. With money this problem never arises because everyone always wants money. Consequently, the

resources used to facilitate exchanges can be put to more productive use.

2. **Unit of Value**—We use our monetary unit as the standard measure of value. We say a shirt is worth $25.00, not 14 chickens.

3. **Store of Value**—Money is one of the forms in which wealth can be stored. Alternatives include stocks and bonds, real estate, gold, works of art, and many others. One advantage of storing wealth in money form is that money is the most **liquid** of all assets. **Liquidity** refers to the ease with which an asset can be transformed into spendable form. Money is already in spendable form. The disadvantage of holding wealth in money form is that money typically pays a lower return than other assets.

4. **Standard of Deferred Payment**—Money is used in transactions involving payments to be made at a future date. An example would be building contracts where full payment is made only when the project is completed. This function of money is implicit in the three already discussed.

What Serves As Money?—Virtually anything can and has served as money. Gold, silver, shells, boulders, cheap metal, paper, and electronic impulses stored in computers are examples of the varied forms money has taken. The only requirement is that the item be generally acceptable. Money does **not** have to have intrinsic value (see below). Typically the items that have served as money have had the following additional characteristics[1]:

1. durability

2. divisibility

3. homogeneity (uniformity or standardization)

4. portability (high value-to-weight and value-to-volume)

5. relative stability of supply

6. optimal scarcity

1. Ralph T. Byrns and Gerald W. Stone, *Macroeconomics*, 3rd edition, (Scott, Foresman and Company, 1987), p. 228.

What Makes Money Valuable?—The rule of money is derived from its acceptance as a medium of exchange. Why can it be exchanged for something useful? Sellers accept money because they know they can use it anywhere else in the country to buy goods and services and pay off debts. If they could not do that, they would not want it. What this means is that the substance that is used for money need not be valuable, and that money need not be backed by anything valuable. Such is the case. Our money is not backed by gold, silver, or anything else. It is just cheap metal, cheap paper, and electronic impulses stored in computers.

Problem Solving Example:

Q What are the functions of money?

A First, money serves us as a medium of exchange. Suppose Mr. Kastner would like to have some tobacco but can only offer philosophy books in return. Now Mr. Voelkle, the owner of a cigar shop, can offer Mr. Kastner some tobacco, but has no desire to read philosophy. Therefore no exchange will take place unless each man has something that the other man will trade for. When money is introduced as a medium of exchange, it provides a solution. Mr. Kastner can sell his books for money on the outside and then spend the proceeds from the sale to buy tobacco at Mr. Voelkle's store. No longer is there any need for the two men to be restricted to making only exchanges of goods and services. Instead, Mr. Kastner will pay an amount of money for a good (tobacco).

Money also serves us as a measure of value. Just as scales measure weights in pounds and ounces, money measures value in dollars and cents. Suppose in the preceding example, Mr. Voelkle agreed to accept philosophy books for his tobacco. Just how much tobacco is equivalent in exchange for the complete works of Nietzsche? The use of money alleviates this problem of measurement.

Money is also a store of value. If Mr. Kastner sells his books, he need not go right out and buy a tremendous amount of tobacco. Rather he can save a portion of it to purchase tobacco in the future. The money saved represents purchasing power deferred to the future.

12.2 The United States' Money Supply

While there are many different definitions of the money supply available, the two most commonly used are M1 and M2.

M1—M1 consists of currency, demand deposits, other checkable deposits, and traveler's checks.

> *Currency*—coins and paper money.

> *Demand deposits*—These are checking accounts held in commercial banks. Funds can be transferred from person to person by means of a check. Demand deposits are considered money because checks are generally acceptable.

> *Other checkable deposits*—This category includes all other financial institution deposits upon which checks can be written. Among these are NOW accounts, ATS accounts, and credit union share drafts.

> *Traveler's checks*—Most traveler's checks are generally acceptable throughout much of the world.

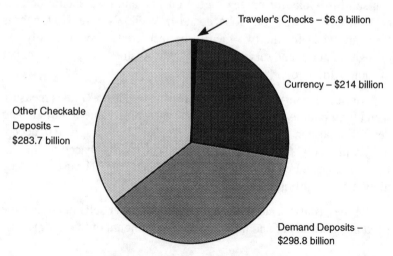

Figure 12.1 Composition of M1x

(Pie chart labels:)
Traveler's Checks – $6.9 billion
Currency – $214 billion
Other Checkable Deposits – $283.7 billion
Demand Deposits – $298.8 billion

Figure 12.1 Composition of M1x

M2—This definition includes all of M1 along with savings deposits, small denomination time deposits, money market mutual funds and deposit accounts, overnight Repo's, and Eurodollars.

Savings Deposits—These are the common passbook savings accounts. They do not provide check writing privileges.

Small Denomination time deposits—A better-known name is certificates of deposits (CD's). They typically do not provide check writing privileges.

Money market mutual funds and deposit accounts—Both mutual funds and deposit accounts are investment funds. Large numbers of people pool their money to allow for diversification and professional investment management. Mutual funds are managed by private financial companies. Deposit accounts are managed by commercial banks. Investors earn a return on their investment and have limited check-writing privileges.

Overnight Repo's and Eurodollars—Overnight Repo's stand for overnight repurchase agreements. Essentially, these are short-term (overnight) loans. A corporation with excess cash may arrange to purchase a security from a bank with the stipulation that the bank will buy the security back the next day at a slightly higher price. The corporation receives a return on its money, and the bank gets access to funds. Eurodollars are dollar-denominated demand deposits held in banks outside the United States (not just in Europe). From the standpoint of M2, deposits held in Caribbean branches of Federal Reserve member banks are relevant. These deposits are easily accessed by U.S. residents. While both items are important in financial affairs, together they are a negligible proportion of M2.

A significant proportion of M2 cannot be used as a medium of exchange. Why, then, are the items considered money? First, each of these items is highly liquid. Second, studies indicate that people's economic behavior is not very sensitive to their relative holdings of the various assets in question.

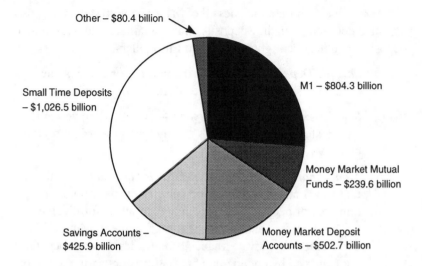

Figure 12.2 Composition of M2

Problem Solving Examples:

What are the three sources of money creation?

The United States Treasury in collaboration with the Federal Reserve issues coins and currency. The Federal Reserve Banks and the commercial banks create demand deposits, or "checkbook money," and time or savings deposits.

Two definitions of money supply are M1 and M2. Differentiate between the two.

M1 is comprised of coin and currency held by the (non-bank) public, and demand deposits in commercial banks. This is the money supply narrowly defined. M2, on the other hand, includes all of

M1 plus time and saving deposits. M2 represents the broader definition of money supply.

12.3 The Financial System

Financial Intermediaries—Financial intermediaries are organizations such as commercial banks, savings and loan institutions, credit unions, and insurance companies. They play an important role in facilitating the saving and investment process which helps the economy grow. Savers typically look to place their money where the combination of return, liquidity, and safety is best. Through the various types of deposits they offer, financial intermediaries compete for the saved funds. The money so obtained is used to finance borrowing. Through their ability to obtain large pools of money from many depositors, intermediaries are able to service the needs of large borrowers.

Balance Sheet of Typical Bank

Assets	Liabilities
Reserves	Demand Deposits
Loans	Savings Deposits
Securities	Time Deposits
Property	Other Deposits
Other Assets	Net Worth

Reserves—Reserves are a bank's money holdings. Most reserves are held in the form of demand deposits at other banks or the Federal Reserve System (see 13.1). The remainder is cash in the bank's vault. Reserves are held to meet the demand for cash on the part of depositors, and to honor checks drawn upon the bank. The amount of reserves a bank must hold is based on the **required reserve ratio**. Set by the Federal Reserve System, the required reserve ratio is a number from 0 to 1.00 and determines the level of reserve holdings relative to the bank's deposits.

Required Reserves—Required reserves are the amount a bank is legally obligated to hold. Required reserves are calculated by multiplying the required reserve ratio by the amount of deposits.

Required Reserves = required reserve ratio × deposits

The required reserve ratio does not make banks safe. In the absence of a requirement, most banks would voluntarily hold adequate reserves to be "safe." In fact, the level of reserves banks are required to hold is probably higher than what they need to be safe. The main purpose of the requirement is to give the Federal Reserve System some control over the banks (see 13.1.4.b).

Excess Reserves—Excess reserves are the difference between the amount of reserves a bank holds and what it is required to hold.

All banks hold excess reserves at all times for reasons of financial prudence, however greater excess reserves will be held during periods of financial uncertainty.

Excess Reserves = Reserves − Required Reserves

Why Can Banks Hold "Fractional" Reserves?—All banks constantly operate with reserve holdings only a fraction of deposit liabilities. This is known as **fractional reserve banking**. If all depositors tried to withdraw their money simultaneously, banks would not be able to honor the demands. Fortunately, this is unlikely to happen because people like to hold deposits because they are safe and convenient. On a normal business day, some withdrawals are made, but these are counterbalanced by new deposits. Reserve holdings need only be a small fraction of deposits for prudent operation.

Problem Solving Examples:

Describe a commercial bank's balance sheet.

The balance sheet of a bank, like that of any firm, is a statement which lists, on the one side, all the categories of "assets," claims owned by the bank, with their monetary values, and, on the other side, all categories of claims against the bank, "liabilities," with their monetary values; and the net worth of the bank, which is simply defined as the difference (positive, negative, or zero) between the total value of assets and the total value of liabilities. Thus total assets are always "balanced" by total liabilities plus net worth, i.e., Assets = Liabilities + Net Worth, since Net Worth = Assets − Liabilities by definition.

A bank's assets are principally the cash it receives from depositors, the loans it has made and expects to be repaid, and the securities (bonds, etc.) it has bought with a part of the cash received from depositors. Its liabilities (ignoring the possibility of time deposits) consist of the demand accounts which it created for depositors upon receipt of their cash and which it is liable to redeem in cash on demand.

A major difference between the balance sheet of a commercial bank and that of a solvent non-bank firm is that the bank's "current liabilities," i.e., those which are due to be met immediately, as the bank's demand deposits are, exceed the value of their "current assets," i.e., those assets which can be immediately converted to cash. Conversely, a solvent non-bank firm has on hand enough assets which are immediately convertible to cash to meet present obligations. If all depositors at once demanded that a bank redeem their accounts in cash, the bank would be unable (without a loan from the Fed) to do so. Part of the depositors' cash is out on loan and thus not available to the bank until the loan is due to be paid back. However, because the current liabilities of banks (checkbook money) are a generally accepted means of payment whereas the IOU's of non-bank firms are not, banks, unlike non-bank firms, are not generally called upon to meet all their current liabilities at once in cash. Thus, they do not face insolvency as long as the public is confident enough in the bank's ability to redeem its deposit accounts in cash on demand to leave its cash in the bank.

 What are "required reserves"? What are "actual reserves" and "excess reserves"?

"Required reserves" are those funds which a commercial bank must keep, either in cash or on account with the Federal Reserve Bank, and which it may not lend out. The amount of a bank's required reserves is a certain percentage, called the required reserve ratio, of its demand (and time) deposits specified by the Federal Reserve.

"Actual reserves" are the funds which a commercial bank possesses at any given time in the form either of cash or balances in its account with the Federal Reserve Bank.

"Excess reserves" is the difference (positive, negative, or zero) between a commercial bank's "actual reserves" and its "required reserves." A commercial bank with positive excess reserves is in a position to increase its loans; a bank with negative excess reserves must decrease the amount it is lending; a bank with zero excess reserves is "loaned up," and may not increase its lending any further, although it may reduce the amount of its loans if it wishes.

12.4 The Money Creation Process

Assume M1 consists of currency and demand deposits only. The banking system consists of many small banks. The required reserve ratio is .20, and all banks are "loaned up" (no bank holds excess reserves). The balance sheet for a "typical" bank, Bank A, and the nation's money supply are shown below. Throughout let R = reserves, L = loans, DD = demand deposits, and NW = net worth.

Bank A		Nation's Money Supply	
R 10,000	DD 50,000	DD =	1,000,000
L 90,000	NW 50,000	Currency =	200,000
		M1 =	1,200,000

Assume an individual deposits $1,000 in cash in Bank A. Note that the nation's money supply does not change, but its composition does.

Bank A		Nation's Money Supply	
R 11,000	DD 51,000	DD =	1,001,000
L 90,000	NW 50,000	Currency =	199,000
		M1 =	1,200,000

Bank A's required reserves are now .20 × 51,000 = 10,200, meaning it has excess reserves of 800. It will move to lend out this money because excess reserves do not earn a return. Note that the nation's money supply will increase as a result of this.

Bank A		Nation's Money Supply	
R 11,000	DD 51,800	DD =	1,001,800
L 90,800	NW 50,000	Currency =	199,000
		M1 =	1,200,800

Presumably the money will be quickly spent and deposited in another bank, Bank B. Bank B will collect on the check from Bank A, frequently using the Federal Reserve System as intermediary.

After the check has cleared, the balance sheets of A and B will look as follows. (Bank B's balance sheet only shows changes in the categories.) Note that check clearing will not affect the size of the nation's money supply, only those banks of which it is the liability.

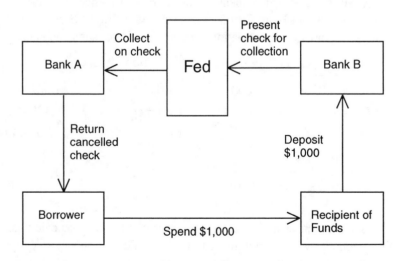

Figure 12.3 The Check Clearing Process

Bank A			Nation's Money Supply	
R 10,200	DD 51,000		DD =	1,001,800
L 90,800	NW 50,000		Currency =	199,000
			M1 =	1,200,800

Bank B	
R +800	DD + 800

Bank B now is holding excess reserves of 640, which it will move to lend out. This will cause the nation's money supply to increase by an additional 640.

Bank B			Nation's Money Supply	
R +800	DD +1,440		DD =	1,002,440
L +640			Currency =	199,000
			M1 =	1,201,440

Assuming the loan is spent by the writing of a check that the recipient deposits in Bank C, the balance sheets of Banks B and C will change as shown while the nation's money supply remains unchanged.

Bank B			Nation's Money Supply	
R +800	DD +800		DD =	1,002,440
L +640			Currency =	199,000
			M1 =	1,201,440

Bank C	
R +640	DD +640

Bank C is now holding excess reserves of 512 (can you calculate this amount?), which it will move to lend out. The nation's money supply will expand by the amount of the loan.

Bank C		Nation's Money Supply	
R +640	DD +1,152	DD =	1,002,952
L +512		Currency =	199,000
		M1 =	1,201,952

The process will continue in a similar manner incorporating more and more banks (some banks may enter the process more than once). The chart summarizes the process:

Summary Chart

Bank	New Demand Deposits	New Required Reserves	New Loans	Cumulative New Demand Deposits (from second col.)
A	1,000	200	800	1,000
B	800	160	640	1,800
C	640	128	512	2,440
D	512	102.40	409.60	2,952
All other banks	2,048	409.60	1638.40	5,000
Totals	5,000	1,000	4,000	

An important conclusion is that the initial deposit of $1,000 allowed the banking system to expand deposit liabilities by $5,000. The formula to calculate this is given in the box below.

$$\Delta DD = 1/r \times \Delta R$$

The expression $(1/r)$, where r is the required reserve ratio, is known as the **deposit expansion multiplier**.

It is important to note that this multiple expansion of the money supply was a product of the actions of all the banks in the banking system. No single bank lent out more than its excess reserves.

Why did each bank restrict itself to lending out its excess reserves?—As a general rule, banks will limit their lending to no more than their excess reserves. Consider what could have happened if Bank A itself had based its lending on the deposit expansion multiplier formula and lent out $4,000.

Bank A

R 11,000	DD 55,000
L 94,000	NW 50,000

After the $4,000 had been spent and the check cleared, Bank A's balance sheet would have changed to:

Bank A

R 7,000	DD 51,000
L 94,000	NW 50,000

Bank A would no longer be meeting its required reserve ratio and would be in severe financial stress. It would also be subject to penalties imposed by the Federal Reserve System. This event can be avoided if banks restrict themselves to lending out no more than their excess reserves.

Real World Complications—In the real world, the deposit expansion multiplier is unlikely to be as large as the value given by the formula. There are three reasons for this:

1. Every bank holds some excess reserves.

2. Some of the new money created leaks out into cash and is not redeposited in a bank.

3. Some bank customers seek deposits other than checking accounts.

Problem Solving Examples:

 What features of commercial banking make banks unique among financial institutions in their ability to expand the money supply?

The money supply (M1) is defined as demand deposits and currency held by the public. Commercial banks alone provide demand deposit accounts subject to withdrawal by check in exchange for deposits of cash or checks. If they simply provided the public with the convenience of accounts subject to withdrawal by check and storage of its cash, however, commercial banks' operations could neither add to nor subtract from the total quantity of money. Deposits into or withdrawals from checking accounts would change the composition but not the quantity of the stock of money.

It is the practice of banks of keeping only a fraction of their deposits on reserve and lending the remainder that enables commercial banks to create money. Loans made by one bank are withdrawn from it and generally deposited in whole or in part, in other banks, adding to total bank deposits. Thus, due to banks' practice of keeping only a fraction of deposits on reserve to cover withdrawals from their demand accounts, and lending out the remainder, a $1 deposit of cash into a checking account reduces total currency holdings by $1 but increases total checking account balances by more than $1, and thus increases the total quantity of money in the economy (currency plus checking account balances).

 What is meant by the term "monetary (or demand deposit) multiplier," and how is it calculated?

The monetary multiplier is the ratio of total demand deposits in the banking system to the total reserves of the system. It is also the multiple of an increase (decrease) in the system's reserves by which the amount of demand deposits in the system expands (contracts) as a result of the increase (decrease) in reserves.

The money multiplier, barring "leakages" of reserves into excess reserve holdings of banks or into the cash holdings of the public, is always the reciprocal of the required, reserve ratio, r, i.e., $\dfrac{1}{r}$. If banks decide to hold excess reserves equal to a certain proportion, e, of their demand deposits, the effect on the money multiplier is the same as that of required reserves held by the bank so that the money multiplier is $\dfrac{1}{r+e}\left(<\dfrac{1}{r}\right)$ the reciprocal of the sum of the required reserve ratio and the excess reserve ratio. Both categories of reserves reduce in the same manner the lending capacity, and thereby the deposit creating capacity of the banking system, from what it would be if banks kept no reserves, but lent them all out.

Quiz: Fiscal Policy Issues— Money and Banking

1. In determining the government's fiscal posture, one should look at

    (A) the actual surplus or deficit.

    (B) the full-employment budget surplus or deficit.

    (C) the personal income tax.

    (D) the inflationary impact which the automatic stabilizers have in full employment economy.

2. Economists are in general agreement that discretionary fiscal policy will stabilize the economy most when

    (A) the budget is balanced each year.

    (B) budget deficits are continuously incurred.

     (C)   deficits are incurred during recessions and surpluses during inflations.

     (D)   deficits are incurred during inflations and surpluses during recessions.

3.   A large public debt may

     (A)   impair incentives to innovate and invest.

     (B)   decrease inflationary pressures in a full-employment economy.

     (C)   shift the consumption schedule down.

     (D)   create a larger stock of private capital for future generations.

4.   The value of money depends on

     (A)   the cost of producing it.

     (B)   the amount of gold the government backs each dollar with.

     (C)   how much each dollar will buy.

     (D)   what the government says each dollar is worth.

5.   The money supply in the U.S. is backed by

     (A)   government bonds.

     (B)   gold in the Fed's vaults.

     (C)   gold and silver in a one to one ratio.

     (D)   the government's ability to keep the dollar's value stable by controlling the money supply.

6. The largest portion of M2 is

    (A) cash.

    (B) government bonds.

    (C) demand deposits.

    (D) time deposits.

7. A bank's assets include its

    (A) loans and deposits.

    (B) net worth and reserves.

    (C) reserves and loans.

    (D) deposits only.

8. A bank's deposits are

    (A) liabilities.

    (B) assets.

    (C) net worth.

    (D) reserves.

9. A bank's excess reserves are

    (A) deposits minus required reserves.

    (B) actual reserves minus loans.

    (C) actual reserves minus required reserves.

    (D) deposits minus loans.

10. If the required reserve ratio is 10%, a bank with $800,000 in deposits and $75,000 in excess reserves has actual reserves of

    (A) $7,500.

    (B) $80,000.

    (C) $5,000.

    (D) $155,000.

ANSWER KEY

1.	(B)		6.	(C)
2.	(C)		7.	(C)
3.	(A)		8.	(A)
4.	(C)		9.	(C)
5.	(D)		10.	(D)

CHAPTER 13

Monetary Policy

13.1 The Federal Reserve System

The Federal Reserve System (known affectionately as the "Fed") is the central bank of the United States. Its responsibilities are to oversee the stability of the banking system and conduct monetary policy to the end of fighting inflation and unemployment and stimulating economic growth.

Structure—The Fed has an unusual structure. It consists of a Board of Governors, twelve regional banks, many subregional banks, and commercial banks that opt for membership in the system. Although created by an act of Congress (in 1913), nominally the Fed is privately owned by the member banks. Members of the Board of Governors are appointed by the president and confirmed by the Senate for 14-year terms. The chair of the board is appointed by the president and confirmed by the Senate for a four-year term. The Fed's budget is overseen by a committee of Congress and it must report to Congress about its operations at least twice a year. To a large extent, the Fed can be considered an independent agency of the government.

The Fed's virtual independence has led to a continuing controversy. Is it wise to give the power to influence the state of the economy to a group who are not directly accountable to the people? The "pro" side claims the Fed's independence puts it "above" politics and leads to decisions more in the "public interest." The "con" side says that in a democracy, the people should be given a voice in all decisions that affect them.

Functions—The major functions of the Fed are as follows:

1. **Bank Regulation**—The Fed has been given the responsibility of examining member banks to determine if they are financially strong and in conformity with the banking regulations. The Fed also approves mergers.

2. **Clearing Interbank Payments**—As shown in Chapter 12, the Fed performs a service for member banks in operating the check clearing function. Banks receiving deposit checks drawn on other banks can present them to the Fed. The Fed will credit the receiving bank's reserve account, reduce the paying bank's reserve account, and send the check back to the paying bank. Banks do not universally avail themselves of this service. Local banks will frequently cooperate and establish their own check clearing process for local checks.

3. **Lender of Last Resort**—One of the original motivations for establishing the Fed was to have a bank that could act as a "lender of last resort."

Bank panics refer to situations where depositors lose faith in their bank and try to withdraw their money. Given the fractional reserve nature of modern banking, it is impossible for all depositors to withdraw their money simultaneously. Failure of depositors to withdraw their from one bank has the potential to scaring other depositors and starting a "run on the banks." By standing ready to loan reserves to banks experiencing difficulties, the Fed helps reduce the danger of panics.

Panics were much more common in the days before the Fed and **Federal Deposit Insurance**, but are not unknown today. Witness the situations with savings and loan institutions in Ohio and Maryland within the last few years.

FEDERAL DEPOSIT INSURANCE

Established during the New Deal era, Federal Deposit Insurance provides government guarantees for bank deposits should a bank fail. Both commercial banks and savings and loans are insured.

4. **Monetary Policy—**

a. **Open Market Operations**—Open market operations refers to the Fed's buying or selling of U.S. government bonds in the open market. The purpose is to influence the amount of reserves in the banking system, and, consequently, the banking system's ability to extend credit and create money.

1. *To expand the economy*—The Fed would buy bonds in the open market. If $50 million in bonds was purchased directly from commercial banks, the banks' balance sheet would change as follows:

All Commercial Banks

R	+ 50 million	
Bonds	– 50 million	

Banks are now holding an additional $50 million in excess reserves which they can use to extend additional credit. To induce borrowers, banks are likely to lower interest rates and credit standards. As loans are made, the money supply will expand as explained in Chapter 12. The additional credit will stimulate additional spending, primarily for investment goods.

The $50 million in bonds could be purchased directly from private individuals. The private individuals would then deposit the proceeds in their bank accounts. After the money was deposited, the balance sheet of all commercial banks would look as follows:

All Commercial Banks			
R	+ 50 million	DD	+ 50 million

As above, the banks are now holding excess reserves which they can use to extend credit. Lower interest rates, a greater money supply, and a higher level of total expenditure will result.

2. *To contract the economy*—The Fed would sell bonds in the open market. If it sold $20 million in bonds directly to the commercial banks, the banks' balance sheet would change as follows:

All Commercial Banks		
R	– 20 million	
Bonds	+ 20 million	

Banks are now deficient in reserves. They need to reduce their demand deposit liabilities, and will do so by calling in loans and making new credit more difficult to get. Interest rates will rise, credit requirements will be tightened, and the money supply will fall. Total spending in the economy will be reduced.

If the Fed sells the $20 million in bonds directly to private individuals, payment will be made with checks drawn against the private individuals' bank accounts. The banks' balance sheet will change as follows:

All Commercial Banks			
R	– 20 million	DD	– 20 million

Again, banks are deficient in reserves. They are forced to reduce credit availability, which will raise interest rates, reduce the money supply, and lead to a drop in total spending.

A Primer on Bonds

Bonds are a financial instrument frequently used by government and business as a way to borrow money. Every bond comes with a par value (often $1,000), a date to maturity (ranging from 90 days to 30 years), a coupon (a promise to pay a certain amount of money each year to the bondholder until maturity), and a promise to repay the par value on the maturity date. The issuing government or business sells the bonds in the bond market for a price determined by supply and demand. The money received from the sale represents the principal of the loan, the annual coupon payment is the interest on the loan, and the principal is repaid at the date of maturity. There is also a secondary market in bonds.

Assume a bond carries a coupon of $100 and is sold for $1,000. Then the annual yield to the purchaser is roughly 10% ($100/$1,000). If the same bond was sold for $950, the yield would be roughly 10.5% ($100/$950). If the same bond was sold for $1,050, the yield would roughly be 9.5% ($100/$1,050). Note the inverse relationship between bond yield and price. Also note that the actual yield formulas are considerably more complicated than those used.

b. **Reserve Ratio**—The Fed can set the legal reserve ratio for both member and non-member banks. The purpose is to influence the level of excess reserves in the banking system, and consequently, the banking system's ability to extend credit and create money.

1. *To expand the economy*—The Fed would reduce the reserve requirement. Assume the reserve requirement is 8%, and all banks are "all loaned up."

   If the Fed reduces the reserve requirement to 6%, required reserves fall to $30 million, and there are immediately $10 million in excess reserves. Banks will lower the interest rates they charge and credit requirements in an attempt to make more loans. As the loans are granted, the economy's money supply and total spending will rise.

All Commercial Banks			
R	40 million	DD	50 million

2. *To contract the economy*—The Fed would raise the reserve requirement. Assume the reserve requirement is 8%, and all banks are "all loaned up."

All Commercial Banks			
R	40 million	DD	50 million

If the Fed raises the reserve requirement to 10%, required reserves rise to $50 million, and banks are immediately $10 million deficient in reserves. Banks will raise the interest rates they charge and credit requirements to reduce the amount of money borrowed. They may also call in loans. As the loans are reduced, the economy's money supply and total spending will fall.

c. **Discount Rate**—One of the responsibilities of the Fed is to act as a "lender of last resort." Member banks needing reserves can borrow from the Fed. The interest rate the Fed charges on these loans is called the **discount rate**. By changing the discount rate, the Fed can influence the amount member banks try to borrow, and, consequently, the banking system's ability to extend credit and create money.

1. *To expand the economy*—The Fed would lower the discount rate. A lower discount rate would make it less "painful" for member banks to borrow from the Fed. Consequently, they will be more willing to lend money and hold a low level of excess reserves. A lower discount rate would lead to lower interest rates and credit requirements, a higher money supply, and greater total spending in the economy.

2. *To contract the economy*—The Fed would raise the discount rate. A higher discount rate would make it more "painful" for member banks to borrow from the Fed. Consequently, they will be less willing to lend money and more likely to hold a high level of excess reserves. A higher discount rate would

lead to higher interest rates and more stringent credit requirements, a lower money supply, and lower total spending in
the economy.

Tool	Action	Effect on Interest Rates	Effect on Money Supply	Effect on Total Spending	Effect on GNP
Open Market	buy	lower	raise	raise	raise
Operations	sell	raise	lower	lower	lower
Reserve	raise	raise	lower	lower	lower
Ratio	lower	lower	raise	raise	raise
Discount	raise	raise	lower	lower	lower
Rate	lower	lower	raise	raise	raise

Table 13.1 Monetary Policy Summary

Problem Solving Examples:

Q What are the primary functions of the Federal Reserve Banks?

A First, the Federal Reserve System has the exclusive legal right
to issue legal tender currency. No commercial bank may
issue currency.

Second, the "Fed" sets the legal reserve requirements for commercial banks. That is, it determines the proportion of deposits that each
commercial bank must keep "in reserve" to cover withdrawals by depositors, and thus also the proportion which each bank may lend out.
The authority to set reserve requirements gives the Fed power to control the maximum quantity of money and credit in the economy.

Third, the Fed acts as the commercial banks' bank, providing accounts in which commercial banks may keep their reserves. It also clears interbank checks like the way in which a commercial bank clears checks between its depositors.

Fourth, it can provide loans to commercial banks, whose reserves fall to inadequate levels, e.g., due to large unexpected withdrawals.

Fifth, the Fed performs most of the federal government's banking services, holding part of the Treasury's revenues, and assisting in tax collection and bond sale and redemption.

Sixth, the Fed plays a role along with state and national governments in regulating the operation of its member commercial banks.

Q The Federal Reserve's most important control instrument is open-market operations. How is it that selling government bonds can reduce bank reserves?

A Suppose the Federal Open Market Committee (FOMC) decides to sell $2 billion of government bonds. To accomplish this, the bonds are sold on the open market. The buyer will most likely pay for the bonds by a check drawn on his bank account. When the Fed presents this check for payment to the bank, the bank will lose an equivalent amount of reserve balances with the Federal Reserve.

So reserves go down by $2 billion. But the process doesn't stop here. Due to the multiple contraction of money, a drop of $2 billion in reserves tends to set off a $10 billion contraction of demand deposits (assuming a reserve requirement of 20% and no leakages).

13.2 The Demand For Money

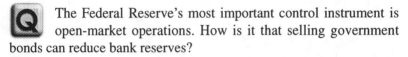

The convenience of money creates a demand for it. By this it is meant that households will choose to hold a certain portion of their wealth in money form. The convenience is primarily its liquidity (See 12.1). Money can be used to buy goods and services, acquire other assets, and provide a cushion against emergencies.

A household's demand for money is **positively related to its**

income (households with higher incomes spend more money, and, consequently, need to hold more money to finance those transactions), and **negatively related to the interest rate** (higher interest rates [i.e., higher returns on assets other than money] increase the opportunity cost of holding wealth in money form because money typically pays no or very low interest).

The demand curve for money can be represented by D1. At higher levels of income, the demand curve will shift out to D2. At lower levels of income, the demand curve will shift in to D3.

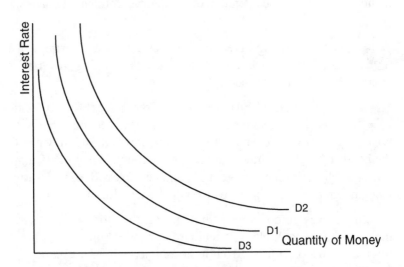

Figure 13.1 The Demand for Money Schedule

13.3 Transmission Mechanism For Monetary Policy

Federal Reserve System actions influence the economy primarily by influencing interest rates, credit availability, and the money supply, and consequently, the interest rate sensitive portion of total spending (mainly, investment).

$$\uparrow MS \rightarrow \downarrow i \rightarrow \uparrow I \rightarrow \uparrow C + I + G + (X - M)$$

$$\downarrow MS \rightarrow \uparrow i \rightarrow \downarrow I \rightarrow \downarrow C + I + G + (X - M)$$

Graphically, an increase in the money supply from MS to MS´ will cause the equilibrium level of GNP to rise to GNP´. A decrease in the money supply from MS to MS´´ will cause the equilibrium level of GNP to fall to GNP´´.

13.4 Monetarism

Monetarism is a school of thought within the economics profession. It is closely related to classical economics. The leading monetarist is Milton Friedman.

Equation of Exchange—The equation of exchange is written as

$$MV = PQ$$

where M = money supply, V = velocity of money (the rate at which money changes hands), P = the average price level, and Q = the quantity of goods and services. The equation says if you multiply the money supply by the rate at which money changes hands, you will get the value of goods and services sold (or the level of income, which is the same thing).

The equation exchange is true by definition. To see that, realize that three dollars in income is created if one dollar changes hands three times. Every time the dollar changes hands, a dollar in income will be created; so if you multiply the one dollar ($1) by the number of times it changes hands (3), you will get the amount of income created ($3).

Velocity of Money—As indicated above, the velocity of money measures the rate at which money changes hands. We cannot trace the movements of dollars in the economy the way we can trace birds by banding their legs, but we do not need to. Simple arithmetic shows that

$$V = \frac{PQ}{M}$$

Using available data on GNP ($4,100 billion in a recent year) and the money supply (M1 = $800 billion in the same year), the velocity of money was $4,100/$800 = 5.125.

Quantity Theory of Money—The quantity theory of money was used by classical economists to explain the rate of inflation. From the equation of exchange, assume that V is constant due to institutional reasons, and Q is constant because the economy's equilibrium is at full employment. Then if M doubles, P must also double. Therefore, the price level is determined by the quantity of money.

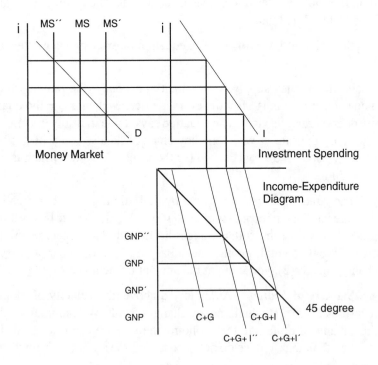

Figure 13.2 Effect of Changes in Money Supply on GNP

Tenets of Modern Monetarism—Modern day monetarists have modified the quantity theory of money. They recognize that Q may not be at the full employment level for extended periods of time. Also, they recognize that V is not a constant, but they believe that V is "relatively stable." This means that V does not change dramatically from year to year, and can be predicted with a relatively small margin of error. If so, then the money supply can be used to predict GNP (PQ) with a high degree of accuracy.

The most important beliefs of the modern monetarists are as follows:

1. Changes in the money supply are the most important factors affecting the economy.
2. The Fed should **not** use discretionary monetary policy in an attempt to stabilize the economy. This may seem contradictory with 1, but it really is not. The monetarists, as a rule, are economic conservatives. They believe the private sector of the economy tends to be relatively stable. Government actions are primarily to blame for economic difficulties. An activist monetary policy would create more problems than it would solve.

The reason for this is because monetary policy actions only affect the economy with a lag. The lag could be well over one year. Consequently, the only way the Fed could follow the appropriate policy today is if it were to know what the economy would be like in a year. Unfortunately, but truthfully, economists are not very apt at forecasting the economy. Thus, the Fed is as likely to follow inappropriate policy as appropriate policy, as likely to make things worse as better. **The preferred approach of monetarists is for the Fed to let the money supply grow at a constant rate**. Since changes in the money supply are the main factor causing fluctuations in the economy, a smooth rate of growth for money should help smooth the growth of the economy. It is true that this policy will not permit the Fed to respond to major problems, but, again, the Fed's response is as likely to be bad as good. A constant rate of growth of the money supply is superior to any alternative.

Problem Solving Examples:

 What is the Quantity Equation of Exchange and how can it be derived?

 The Quantity Equation of Exchange is the formal identity

$$MV \equiv PQ.$$

P is the average price level, and Q stands for real GNP, which is computed statistically by "deflating" money GNP by the price index. M is the total money supply and V the velocity of circulation of money.

The velocity of money, or income turnover is defined as the ratio of GNP to the money supply.

$$V \equiv \frac{GNP}{M} \equiv \frac{p_1q_1 + p_2q_2 + \dots}{M} \equiv \frac{PQ}{M}$$

When we multiply both sides of this identity by M, we get a new identity, the Quantity Equation of Exchange $MV \equiv PQ$.

Example: the money supply M is about \$290 billion, GNP about \$1,500 billion. So $\frac{GNP}{M} = \frac{1,500}{290} = 5.2$ per year is the income velocity. This means that each unit of money was used for GNP transactions about 5.2 times per year.

Or, differently stated, people hold at average a money balance equivalent to 70 days income.

The principal causes of changes in the velocity appear to be changes in interest, the rate of inflation, and real income; all three affecting the money balances people prefer to hold.

 Define the Quantity Theory of Money.

The theory can be stated as follows: Assuming no change in the volume of goods and services exchanged or the velocity of money circulating, price level variations are directly dependent upon changes in the quantity of money. Symbolically,

$M\overline{V} = P\overline{Q}$, where $\overline{V}$ and $\overline{Q}$ are both constant.

Dividing both sides of the equation by $\overline{Q}$ results in $P = \dfrac{\overline{V}}{\overline{Q}}M = kM$.

Since both $\overline{V}$ and $\overline{Q}$ are constant, and will not change, we can define $k = \dfrac{\overline{V}}{\overline{Q}}$. This crude form of the Quantity Theory of money is useful for the understanding of hyperinflations and long term price increments.

A modern form of the Quantity Theory does not use the levels of the prices and the money supply but the relative rates of change:

$$\frac{\Delta P}{P} = k \cdot \frac{\Delta M}{M}$$

Because k is only a proportionality constant that depends on the units used, it can be omitted for all practical purposes; and the modern version reads

$$\pi = m$$

where π is the rate of change in the general price level (if upward it is called inflation; if downward—deflation), and m is the rate of the money supply.

A more sophisticated form of the Quantity Theory of Money recognizes the fact that the ratio $\dfrac{V}{Q}$ is not constant. It is then assumed, however, that the changes in this ratio are gradual and predictable.

CHAPTER 14

Inflation

14.1 Theory of Inflation

Demand Pull Inflation—"Too much money chasing too few goods" is an apt description of demand pull inflation. More technically, demand pull inflation occurs when the level of spending in the economy exceeds the amount firms are capable of producing. To ration the available goods and services, firms raise prices. Excess demand then pulls up the general price level.

In a simple Keynesian model, inflation is unlikely to occur when the economy is operating below full employment. If there is an increase in spending firms will hire unemployed resources and produce more output. Competition leads firms to respond with output increases rather than price increases. When the economy reaches full employment, firms no longer have the option of increasing output. They must raise prices. The solution to demand pull inflation is to reduce demand.

In Figure 14.1, an increase in aggregate expenditure from AE1 to AE2 will result in higher GNP with no increase in the price level. A further increase to AE3 will only result in higher prices.

Phillips Curve—Named after Australian economist A.W. Phillips, the Phillips Curve was originally a relationship between the level of unemployment and the rate of increase of wages. Since wage increases typically lead to price increases, a natural extension was to look at the relationship between the level of unemployment and the rate of inflation, and this latter relationship was what most economists mean today when they refer to the Phillips Curve.

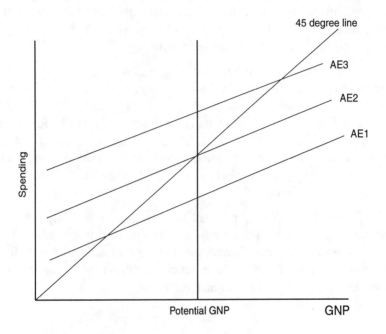

Figure 14.1 Demand–Pull Inflation

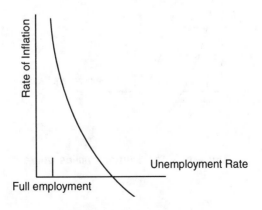

Figure 14.2 The Phillips Curve

There are two significant things about the Phillips Curve. First, it indicates that there is a **trade-off** between inflation and unemployment. Policies that reduce unemployment have a cost in terms of higher inflation. Policies to fight inflation have a cost in terms of higher unemployment. Second, it indicates that inflationary problems can begin before an economy reaches full employment.

An explanation for the second phenomenon is the sectoral inflation theory. According to this theory, as an economy expands out of a recession, some sectors of the economy (i.e., industries) will reach full capacity before others. The sectors at full capacities will be forced to raise prices if expansion continues, while other sectors continue to struggle with used capacity (unemployment). As more sectors reach full capacity (the economy gets nearer to full employment), the inflation rate will increase.

The Phillips Curve appeared to be a good description of the economy's behavior in the 1950s and 1960s. During the 1970s and 1980s it was not as good. Economists have speculated that the Phillips Curve is capable of shifting in or out and it shifted out during the last two decades, giving us a worsened trade-off.

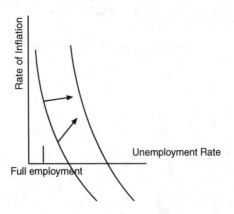

Figure 14.3 The Shifting Phillips Curve

Inflationary Expectations—Inflationary expectations refers to society's beliefs about what is going to happen to the rate of inflation. It is an important concept because inflationary expectations tend to be self-fulfilling. If consumers believe inflation will increase in the future, they are apt to buy more and save less now, contributing to excess demand. If workers believe that inflation is going to increase in the future, they are apt to demand automatic wage increases to protect them and have cost-of-living protections built into labor contracts. Both actions will raise future costs and make inflation more likely. Higher inflationary expectations will shift the Phillips Curve outward. Lower expectations will shift the curve inward. One important goal of economic policy becomes influencing people's expectations.

Accelerationist Hypothesis—Much of the economics profession today believes the long run Phillips Curve is a vertical line at the natural rate of unemployment. This implies there is no permanent trade-off between inflation and unemployment, and that full employment can be achieved and held at any level of inflation, provided people come to expect that rate and adjust accordingly.

Attempts to hold unemployment below the natural rate will lead to accelerating inflation. This is because policies which reduce unemployment (i.e., policies that increase aggregate expenditure) will raise prices and wages and throw markets out of equilibrium. As firms recognize their wage costs have risen, they will be forced to raise prices further. As workers realize the purchasing power of their higher wages has been reduced by higher prices, they will demand still greater wage increases. Inflationary expectations will take hold and wages and prices push each other higher and higher. Only high unemployment for an extended period of time is capable of bringing the inflation rate back to an acceptable level.

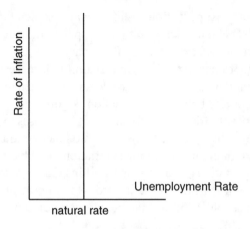

Rate of Inflation

Unemployment Rate

natural rate

Figure 14.4 The Long Run Phillips Curve

Cost Push and Supply Shock Inflation—Both refer to similar situations, when factors on the supply side of the economy push up costs of production and force firms to raise prices. Cost push inflation is the term frequently used when labor unions are deemed the villains in the story. According to the theory, irresponsible unions demand and win "excessive" wage increases which force firms to raise prices. Of course, the price increases become the rationale for a new round of wage increases leading to a **wage-price spiral**. A variation on the story sees the initial push coming from firms that raise prices to raise their profits. These prices are costs to other firms and they also stimulate labor to demand higher wages, and the spiral continues. Supply shock inflation is of more recent vintage. It occurs when a vital resource becomes scarce, causing its price to rise and raising costs of production for firms, setting off an upward spiral. An example of a factor causing supply shock inflation would be oil shortages. Both can be presented graphically by an outward shift of the Phillips Curve. Both create dilemmas for anti-inflation policy because upward movements in costs will also force firms to lay off workers. Thus the economy faces stagflation. If the authorities raise demand to put people back to work, the inflation problem worsens. If the authorities reduce demand to fight inflation, the unemployment problem gets worse.

Problem Solving Examples:

 a) The theory which attributes inflation to excessive wage demands by unions or price demands by large producers is called the _____.

b) The theory which attributes inflation to excessive aggregate demand is called the _____.

Give an explanation of both theories.

a) cost-push theory of inflation
b) demand-pull theory of inflation

The cost-push theory, or cost-price spiral theory of inflation requires the existence of the "ratchet-effect," or stickiness of prices. This means that prices move flexibly upward but are rather "sticky" downward. The union demands for higher wages, backed by the oligopolistic character of the trade unions in the labor market, or the demands for higher prices for oil supplied (a raw material input) by the Oil Producing and Exporting Countries (OPEC is a cartel in the raw material markets), or the autonomous price increases by large industrial producers of intermediate products (for example, of steel) increase the costs of producing. These raised costs are passed on to the consumers in the increased prices of the final products, inducing the general price level to increase. The consumers feel the brunt of inflation by noticing a decline in their purchasing power, (thus in their real income), and will require an increase in their nominal income, i.e., their wages and salaries, etc. This process is circular and leads to the cost-price-spiral (see the first figure on the next page).

If prices were generally flexible and moved easily downward then a reallocation of resources would take place from the unionized and oligopolistic sectors to the non-unionized and more competitive sectors, thus from the controlled sector of the economy to the "uncontrolled" sector of the economy.

The demand-pull theory of inflation states that aggregate demand is bigger than the potential output of the economy, pulling the general price level upward:

$$^Y\text{potential} = \frac{^Y\text{demand}\uparrow}{P\uparrow} = \text{constant}$$

There is an inflationary gap: ^{Y}demand $-^Y$potential. Such an inflationary gap may be caused by an increase in autonomous consumption $\overline{C}$ and investment In, caused by optimistic expectations, new technological developments or lower taxes on business profits.

It may also be caused by fiscal policy: increasing government expenditures, decreasing income taxes, or both, or by monetary policy: increasing the money supply and lowering the interest rates, thereby inducing more investment (see second figure).

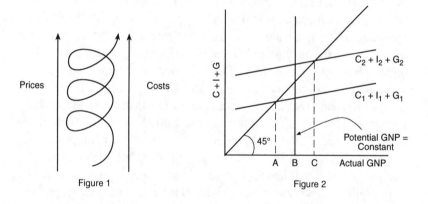

Figure 1

Figure 2

AB is the deflationary gap with unemployment, to be closed by increased spending. BC is the inflationary gap.

Q What is the Phillips Curve? And what is the expectations-augmented Phillips Curve?

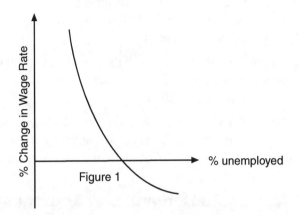

Figure 1

A The Phillips Curve, as conceived by Professor A.W. Phillips of the London School of Economics in the 1950s, was an empirical relationship between the percentage of wage increase and the percentage of unemployment. (See Figure 1) Because of the direct relationship between the percentages of price and wage increase, respectively, it became fashionable in the 1960s to relate the percentage of price increase = inflation rate π to the unemployment rate u (See Figure 2).

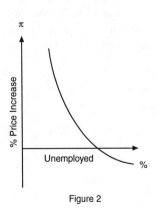

Figure 2

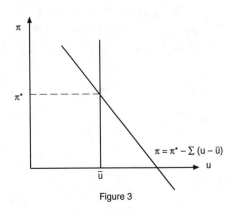

$$\pi = \pi^* - \Sigma (u - \bar{u})$$

Figure 3

In the 1970s the expectations-augmented Phillips Curve was introduced: this is a relationship between actual inflation π, expected (or anticipated) inflation π^*, and the difference between the actual unemployment rate u, and the natural rate of unemployment $\bar{u}$. A linear form of the expectations-augmented Phillips Curve can be presented as $\pi = \pi^* - \varepsilon(u - \bar{u})$. (See Figure 3)

From Figure 3 we notice that when the actual rate of inflation u is equal to the natural rate of inflation $\bar{u}$, $u = \bar{u}$, the actual rate of inflation π equals the expected rate of inflation π^*.

The Phillips Curve is also called the price-job trade-off curve, because a higher rate of inflation is accompanied by a lower rate of unemployment and a lower rate of inflation with more unemployment.

14.2 Aggregate Demand and Aggregate Supply Model

The simple Keynesian model as represented by the Income-Expenditure diagram is not adequate to explain the dynamics of inflation as the United States has experienced it over the last two decades. The Aggregate Demand and Aggregate Supply Model is more enlightening.

Aggregate Demand Schedule—The Aggregate Demand Schedule shows the relationship between the general price level and the real level of spending in the economy.

The negative relationship can be explained this way. A reduction in the general price level increases the real value of consumer wealth, leading to greater spending and hence a higher level of real GNP.

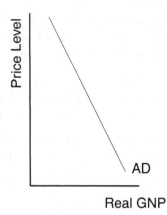

Figure 14.5 The Aggregate Demand Schedule

AD shifts in	AD shifts out
higher taxes on households	lower taxes on households
lower government spending	higher government spending
Fed reduces money supply	Fed increases money supply
reduced consumer confidence	increased consumer confidence
higher corporate taxes	lower corporate taxes

Table 14.1

As a general rule, only events that reduce aggregate expenditure shift the AD schedule in; any event that raises aggregate expenditure will shift AD out. Examples of events that will shift AD are shown in Table 14.1.

Aggregate Supply Schedule—The Aggregate Supply Schedule shows the relationship between the general price level and the amount of real output firms produce.

The positive relationship can be explained this way. A higher price level will stimulate greater production because it offers more opportunity for profit. Alternatively, since greater production will raise costs of production, firms must charge higher prices.

As a general rule, events that raise costs of production will shift AS inward; events reducing costs of production will shift AS outward. Examples of events that will shift AS are shown in Table 14.2.

Equilibrium in the Aggregate Demand/Aggregate Supply Model—The intersection of the AD and AS schedules gives the equilibrium general price level and real GNP. Shifts in either curve will change the equilibrium point.

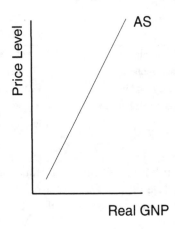

Figure 14.6 The Aggregate Supply Schedule

AS shifts in	AS shifts out
higher inflationary expectations	lower inflationary expectations
"excessive" wage increases	wage "give-backs"
higher taxes on business	lower taxes on business

Table 14.2

Using the Model—The model can be used to predict how the economy will react to various situations.

Increase in AD—Assume AD increases for some reason. Initially the level of real GNP and employment will rise along with the price level. This is the standard Phillips Curve relation. However, several things will happen next. As workers realize that prices have risen, they will demand wage increases to cover the increase in the price level. In addition, their inflationary expectations will increase. Also, firms will observe their costs of production going up both as a result of higher wages and higher material costs. This will cause the AS schedule to shift in. Prices will increase further and output (and employment) will fall unless the authorities react by increasing AD even more, which will cause prices to increase still more and create the conditions for another shift in the AS schedule.

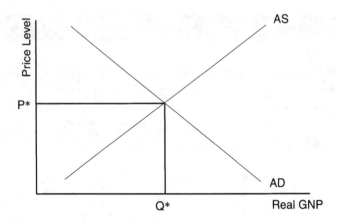

Figure 14.7 Equilibrium in AD/AS Model

Decreases in AS—Assume a supply shock, like an oil embargo. This will shift in the AS schedule leading to both higher prices and lower real GNP (and employment). If the authorities try to restore the lost jobs by raising AD, prices will go still higher. If the authorities try to reduce inflation, real GNP (and employment) will be further reduced.

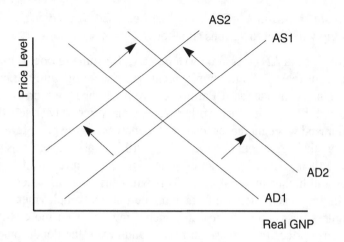

Figure 14.8 Increase in Aggregate Demand

Problem Solving Example:

Q It is observed that attempts by the Federal Reserve to combat inflation have caused output to decline and the rate of unemployment to increase. Can you give a possible explanation of this trade-off between inflation and unemployment within the classical framework of aggregate supply and demand schedules?

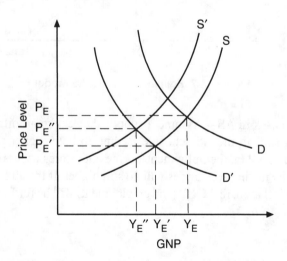

A The basic cause of the trade-off between inflation and cyclical unemployment seems to be the wage and price inflexibilities, caused by the wage policies of the trade unions and the price policies of the business firms. The existence of the system of wage and price contracts provides lags in the reaction patterns of wages and prices. During the expansionary phase of the business cycle, wage increases typically lag behind the increase in aggregate demand, and when the Federal Reserve tightens the money supply to restrict the increase in inflation and aggregate demand falls, wage increases are still trying to catch up with the loss of real income caused by the inflation in the expansionary phase. These wage increases mean increases in production costs of business which is confronted at the same time with a drop in the sales = fall in aggregate demand.

A fall in aggregate demand moves the aggregate demand schedule D (see accompanying figure) to the left to D' causing a slight fall in equilibrium income Y_E to Y'_E, and a drop in equilibrium price P_E to P'_E. An increase in production costs shifts the supply schedule S up to S' because the producers are only willing to supply the same output at a higher price. This upward movement of the supply schedule depresses the equilibrium income even further to Y'_E and pushes the price level up again. The total result is a sharp fall in total output, and thus in employment, and almost no change in the price level.

14.3 Anti-Inflation Policy

Reducing Aggregate Demand—Lowering the money supply or government spending or raising taxes is the classic solution to inflation. Given adequate time, it will always work. Unfortunately, the side effects are sometimes worse than the disease. Using the Phillips Curve idea, reductions in demand will inevitably cause job losses, possibly for extended periods of time if peoples' inflationary expectations take a while to adjust to the new environment. This policy is sometimes called "biting the bullet" or "the old-time religion."

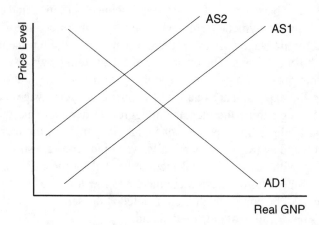

Figure 14.9 Decrease in Aggregate Supply

Rational Expectations—Rational expectations is a relatively new school of thought in the economics profession. It believes that people form inflationary expectations quickly in a rational manner, using all the information available. Its significance in this context is the theory's prediction that inflation is capable of being beaten quickly with limited cost. This will happen if the government has credibility with the public. Thus if the government proclaims an anti-inflationary policy, the public immediately believes it and adjusts its inflationary expectations immediately to an environment of no inflation. Under these circumstances inflation will fall almost instantaneously, and there need be no extended period of high unemployment.

Wage and Price Controls—Economists who believe that inflationary problems stem largely from cost push factors are attracted to wage and price controls as a solution. Under this policy, government decrees limits on how much wages and prices can be raised. This will both directly reduce inflation and also reduce inflationary expectations. Conservative economists believe this cure is worse than the disease because the controls will distort markets, causing artificial shortages of goods and services. The United States has used controls during wartime fairly successfully. A full-fledged system of controls was in effect during part of the Nixon administration. While the controls reduced inflation while they were in effect, many economists believe the post-controls price explosion meant they had no long term positive impact. A mild form of controls was used during the Kennedy-Johnson administration. Wage and price controls are sometimes known as an income policy.

TIP—TIP stands for tax-based income policy. Its purpose is to use the tax system to control wages and prices. A common form is to offer tax reductions to groups of workers and firms who show restraint in their wage and price behavior.

Problem Solving Examples:

 What are some of the ways for government, business, and the consumer to halt or control inflation?

 Government can control the supply of money and credit, thereby avoiding overexpansion of business.

This relates to monetary theory and policy which assumes a direct relationship between the supply of money and aggregate income:

$$Y = f(M)$$

where f( ) denotes a functional relationship, which may be linear

$$Y = k.M$$

thus

$$\Delta Y = k.\Delta M,$$

a reduction in the money supply causes a preferably multiplied reduction in the aggregate demand (k is assumed to be greater than one). Taxes can be increased, thus reducing personal consumption. Increases in the national debt should be avoided and nonessential government expenditures should be reduced.

This relates to the simple Keynesian multiplier theory and fiscal policy, which states a direct relationship between aggregate autonomous spending and aggregate income.

$$Y = \frac{1}{1-c}\left(I + \overline{C} + G - cT\right)$$

Fiscal policy controls government expenditures G and taxes T; $(T - G)$ is the budget deficit financed by issuing government paper (obligations, Treasury Bills, money), thereby contributing to the national debt.

Business can help fight inflation by trying to increase the productivity of workers. This would decrease costs. Construction should be postponed insofar as feasible because this reduces investment in buildings, machinery, and inventory and thereby reduces aggregate demand. Also, production should be geared toward reasonable demand and unnecessary stockpiling of raw materials and semi-finished products should be avoided.

Labor can help fight inflation by also trying to increase productivity and cooperating with management in controlling the wage-price spiral, i.e., not setting excessive wage-bids.

Consumers can help by increasing personal savings, and thus decreasing personal spending, again reducing aggregate demand. Of course, these suggestions look rather flimsy when held up in the light of the real world. For government, before any economic issue can be decided, the political half of the issue must be solved. This often causes government to ignore the economic issue or try to solve it in a roundabout, often unsuccessful manner.

The business world understands that if we were to all work together, inflation could be controlled. But self-interest is the motivating force in the American industrial (capitalist) system, which is highly competitive. In this situation it seems risky to postpone expansion of the production facilities, to keep prices steady and profits low.

Finally, the consumer is confronted by the savings paradox. He/she knows that more savings and less consumption would help fight inflation, but it is inflation itself that is preventing the consumer from saving more, by inducing him/her to spend now.

 When are wage-price controls appropriate and why?

We can best answer this question by stating when wage-price controls are not appropriate. That is when the initial cause of inflation, i.e., excess demand, is not removed. Price-wage controls will ultimately break down into widespread avoidance, public disobedience, and soaring black markets if the excess demand continues. The inflationary gap may be removed by fiscal and monetary policies.

But when the initial cause for inflation is removed and inflation perpetuates in an inflationary spiral, because it is built-in in the economy (inflationary expectations, inflation clauses in contracts), then it is appropriate to apply wage and price controls to change the dynamics of the inflationary process (change the expectations, the clauses). Thus wage-price controls are supplementary to fiscal and monetary policy.

Price and wage controls are difficult and costly to apply: literally tens of thousands of pay scales and hundreds of thousands of commodity prices have to be controlled.

CHAPTER 15

Economic Growth

15.1 Fundamentals of Economic Growth

Productivity—Productivity is a measure of how much output we produce for each hour of work. If a worker is able to produce 10 widgets in an hour's time, then the worker's productivity is 10 widgets per hour. Productivity should not be confused with total output. The relationship between the two is that:

Total Output = Productivity × Number of Hours Worked

If a worker produces 10 widgets per hour and works 40 hours, then total output is 10 widgets per hour × 40 hours = 400 widgets.

Productivity and Living Standards—The key to improving a nation's living standards is to raise productivity. If we can produce more per hour, then more is available to be consumed, we can work fewer hours, or some combination of the two.

Increasing Productivity—There are two main ways to raise productivity. **We can work harder, or we can work smarter**. Working harder refers to expending more effort during each hour of work. It seems unlikely that much of our economy's increase in productivity over time reflects people actually working harder. Working smarter refers to a number of factors, including using more and better capital equipment, better education, more finely developed job skills, and better health. Presumably the bulk of our increase in productivity reflects these factors.

Assume two farm workers are given the task of plowing a ten acre field. Farm worker 1 is given an ox and a plow. Farm worker 2 is given a modern tractor complete with air-conditioned cab and tape deck. It is obvious that 2 will be more productive, but it is unlikely that 2 will have worked "harder." Farm worker 2's higher productivity reflects the fact that he/she has more and better capital to work with and the skills to operate it.

Rule of 72—This is a mathematical rule of thumb that can be applied to growth rates. If you divide the growth rate of anything into 72, you get the approximate amount of time it takes for that thing to double in size.

Time to Double = 72/growth rate

For example, if real GNP grows 3% a year, then it should take approximately 72/3 = 24 years for GNP to double in size.

The rule of 72 is important in talking about productivity growth. From approximately the end of World War II to the late 60s, productivity grew about 3% per year in the United States.

Since that time, it has grown about 1% per year. A two percentage point difference might not seem like much, but if you apply the rule of 72 then the difference is seen to be highly significant. At a 3% growth rate, productivity will double every 24 years, about a generation. At a 1% growth rate, it will take 72 years for productivity to double, about the average life span of an individual. The change in productivity growth rates will cause dramatic differences in future living standards.

Problem Solving Examples:

Q Define productivity of labor and provide an example.

 A Productivity of labor is the amount of output produced by each worker on the average. Thus, if a firm uses 20 workers and 8 units of capital to produce 100 units of output, the productivity of its labor is 5 units. If at a later time a firm changes its input combination to

25 workers and 15 units capital while output rises to 200 units, the new productivity of labor becomes 8 units. One can say that as a result of this change the labor productivity has risen by $\left(\frac{8-5}{5} \cdot 100 = 60 \right)$ 60%.

Q What is the rule of 72?

A In dealing with populations, we often use the so-called "rule of 72." It is used to approximate the doubling time of the population, or of interest. Suppose you estimate that the population of a country will grow at an annual rate of 6% for the next 25 years. To find out when the population will be double its present size, you could use a logarithm table or a calculator. But if neither are handy, you can simply divide the annual growth rate into 72 to approximate the doubling time. Therefore doubling time ~72/6 = 12 years. If we use a calculator, we find that the true answer is 11.8956 years. So we see that the error by using this rule of thumb is slight.

Keep in mind that the rule of 72 can also be used in determining doubling time for interest accounts at banks or in any compound interest situation.

15.2 Supply-Side Economics

Supply-side economics is an approach to economics that places great emphasis on the effect of policies on our willingness to work and ability to produce. In a sense, all economists are "supply-siders" because economic analysis has always stressed the influence of incentives in influencing both consumption and production behavior, but, in the context of the United States, supply-side economics usually refers to the policy views of a group of economists and politicians who have actively promoted above all else the use of tax cuts and deregulation as a method of restoring rapid growth. They believed that marginal tax rates were so high as to dramatically reduce the reward from working, saving, and investing with predictable undesirable results. Likewise, excessive government regulation of business was alleged to be stifling productive activity. These views were ~~y~~ prominent during the administration of President Ronald Reagan.

Laffer Curve—Associated with econom. Arthur Laffer, the Laffer curve (See Figure 15.1) concept almost per~~tly~~ summarizes what supply-side economics is all about. The curve s~~ws~~ the relationship between the marginal tax rate and the government tax revenue.

At a 0% tax rate, the government obviously will ot take in any revenue. At a 100% rate, the government likewise will ~~t~~ take in any revenue because there is no reward for working so no on will work and earn any income. Since the government does tax and ta~~k~~ in some revenue, the curve must have a positively sloped segment, b~~t~~ it also must curve back at some tax rate to reach the point of 0 revenu and 100% tax rate.

While no economist would disagree with the basic logic of the Laffer curve, what supply-side economists did was to take the extra step to imply that American tax rates were so high that the economy was on the negatively sloped portion of the curve. They then advocated tax rate cuts as a way to stimulate higher productivity with the added bonus that the government's revenues would actually increase.

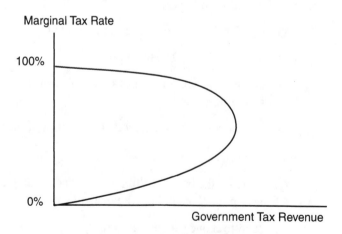

Marginal Tax Rate

Figure 15.1 The Laffer Curve

Quiz: Monetary Policy— Economic Growth

1. Which of the following is not a contractionary policy?

    (A) Raising the discount rate

    (B) Increasing the legal reserve ratio

    (C) Selling bonds

    (D) Persuading commercial banks to approve less loans

2. A tighter money supply

    (A) increases the value of bonds.

    (B) activates private investment.

    (C) causes the interest rate to rise.

    (D) raises the price of bonds.

3. Commercial banks tend to

    (A) just fulfill the reserve ratio requirement.

    (B) often fall below the legal ratio.

    (C) create reserves in excess of legal requirements for safety purposes.

    (D) accept new deposits reluctantly in times of inflation.

4. Lower discount rates

    (A) increase the banks' willingness to lend, as they usually accompany the policy of easing the money supply.

    (B) tend to reduce economic activity.

    (C)   act in the same way a* higher legal reserve ratio.

    (D)   always result in a reducti* in the price of bonds.

5.   The higher the legal reserve ratio

    (A)   the more prone to lending the b*ks are.

    (B)   the larger is the money supply in th* economy.

    (C)   the harder it is for commercial banks to create new money.

    (D)   the more likely inflation is.

6.   As the market interest rate rises

    (A)   government bonds fall in value.

    (B)   government bonds grow in value.

    (C)   the price of government bonds is not affected.

    (D)   people want to hold as much money as possible.

7.   During open-market operations

    (A)   bonds inevitably fall in price.

    (B)   the goals of Federal Reserve often change.

    (C)   bonds are sold to or bought from anonymous customers.

    (D)   many banks fail.

8.   By "cost-push (or sellers') inflation," economists are referring to

    (A)   attempts by labor and industry to set prices and wages that will give them together more than 100 percent of the available product.

(B) rising prices due to excessive levels of government spending financed by open-market operations through the Fed.

(C) rising prices due to excessive levels of aggregate demand.

(D) the rise in total sales revenue attributable to price-tag changes rather than to real volume changes.

9. The basic problem portrayed by the Phillips Curve is

(A) that unemployment tends to increase at the same time the general price level is rising.

(B) that changes in the composition of total labor demand tend to be deflationary.

(C) the possibility that automation will increase the level of noncyclical unemployment.

(D) that a level of aggregate demand sufficiently high to result in full employment may also cause inflation.

10. We speak of demand-pull inflation when

(A) MV is no longer exactly equal or proportional to PQ.

(B) M changes and prices go up.

(C) aggregate demand, prices, and employment are all rising at equivalent rates.

(D) aggregate demand is greater than the value of what the economy can produce at full employment.

ANSWER KEY

1.	(C)	6.	(A)
2.	(C)	7.	(C)
3.	(C)	8.	(A)
4.	(A)	9.	(D)
5.	(C)	10.	(D)

CHAPTER 16

International Economics

16.1 Income-Expenditure Model With Foreign Sector

In the income-expenditure model, international economic transactions affect the economy through their influence on aggregate expenditure. Exports of goods and services represent foreign demand for our output, and add to aggregate expenditure. Imports of goods and services represent a diversion of domestic purchasing power to foreign product. Imports, then, are associated with a reduction in aggregate expenditure. A term representing net exports $(X - M)$ is added to the expression for aggregate expenditure.

$$AE = C + I + G\,(X - M)$$

This simple model ignores international transactions in real and financial assets.

Marginal Propensity to Import—Imports are considered to be induced spending. The level of imports is influenced positively by household income. As household income rises, households buy more goods and services, including those produced in foreign countries. The marginal propensity to import measures the proportion of additional income spent on imports.

$$MPM = \Delta M/\Delta DI$$

Export Multiplier—The export multiplier measures the change in GNP resulting from a $1 change in exports.

$$\text{Export Multiplier} = \Delta GNP / \Delta X$$

The formula is:

$$\text{Export Multiplier} = 1/(1 - MPC + MPM)$$

Impact on other multipliers–Recognition of the foreign sector causes the formulas for the other autonomous expenditure multipliers to be modified.

$$\text{Consumption multiplier} = 1/ (1 - MPC + MPM)$$

$$\text{Investment multiplier} = 1/ (1 - MPC + MPM)$$

$$\text{Government spending multiplier} = 1/ (1 - MPC + MPM)$$

$$\text{Tax multiplier} = (MPM - MPC)/ (1 - MPC + MPM)$$

16.2 International Trade

Why do nations trade with each other?

Principle of Absolute Advantage—A country possesses an absolute advantage in the production of a good or service if it is the most efficient producer of the item. For example, since herring only swim in cold waters and bananas can only grow in warm, moist climates, Norway has an absolute advantage in fishing for herring and Guatemala has an absolute advantage in growing bananas. Norway is better off by devoting resources to fishing and using the herring caught to trade for Guatemalan bananas than trying to grow bananas itself. Likewise with Guatemala.

Law of Comparative Advantage—The law of comparative advantage explains why trade is beneficial between two nations even if one of the nations holds an absolute advantage in the production of all goods and services. In other words, absolute advantage is irrelevant to explaining the pattern of specialization and trade.

Assume a world of two nations of about equal size, called Japan and the United States. They are each capable of producing only two goods, telephones, and VCRs. Resources are fully employed in both nations. Table 16.1 shows total productivity in the production of both goods.

	Telephones per unit of resources	VCRs per unit of resources
Japan	2	6
U.S.	1	1

Table 16.1

Note that Japan has an absolute advantage in the production of both goods. Note also the opportunity costs of production in both countries. (See Table 16.2)

	Cost of One Telephone	Cost of One VCR
Japan	3 VCRs	1/3 telephone
U.S.	1 VCR	1 telephone

Table 16.2

Opportunity costs are computed as follows. In Japan, if one unit of resources is shifted from VCR to telephone production, 6 VCRs must be given up to get 2 telephones. Therefore, 2 T = 6 VCR, or 1 T = 3 VCR. The opportunity cost of good X in terms of good Y is

Y per unit of resources/ X per unit of resources

A country has a comparative advantage in the production of a good if it has the lowest opportunity cost. Here Japan has the comparative advantage in VCRs because they cost only 1/3 telephone as compared to one telephone in the United States. The U.S., despite being less efficient than Japan in telephone production, has a comparative advantage because telephones cost only one VCR as opposed to three in Japan.

As a general rule, regardless of how inefficient a producer a country is, it is bound to have a comparative advantage in something.

Why and what will the Japanese trade with the United States? If the Japanese try to produce telephones, it will cost them three VCRs for every unit of resources shifted to telephone production. It may be cheaper to buy phones in the U.S. where they cost only one VCR. Similarly, domestically produced VCRs cost one telephone in the U.S., but the U.S. may be able to buy them cheaper in Japan, where they only cost 1/3 VCR. Even though Japan has an absolute advantage in the production of telephones, it makes sense for them to buy from the United States. Even though the U.S. lacks an absolute advantage in telephone production, it can be a successful competitor in the world market.

The magnitude of the gains from trade will depend on the world prices that arise for VCRs and telephones. The U.S. may charge Japan more than 1 VCR per phone. As long as the price is less than three VCRs, the Japanese are better off trading for phones than producing them themselves. Likewise with the U.S. and VCRs.

The price of phones and VCRs in the world market (the exchange ratio between phones and VCRs) cannot be determined precisely. We know it must be between 1T = 1VCR and 1T = 3VCR for both countries to be able to benefit from trade.

Regardless of the countless complications that could be added to this model, the lesson of the law of comparative advantage continues to hold.

Gains from specialization—An implication of the law of comparative advantage is that the gains to a nation from specializing and trading exceed the losses. Assume the tables show some of the points on the production possibilities curves for Japan and the United States.

United States

VCRs	30	27	24	21	18	15	12	9	6	3	0
Telephone	0	3	6	9	12	15	18	21	24	27	30

Table 16.3

Japan

VCRs	100	90	80	70	60	50	40	30	20	10	0
Telephone	0	3.3	6.6	10	13.3	16.6	20	23.3	26.6	30	33.3

Table 16.4

Graphs of each country's production possibilities curve are shown below.

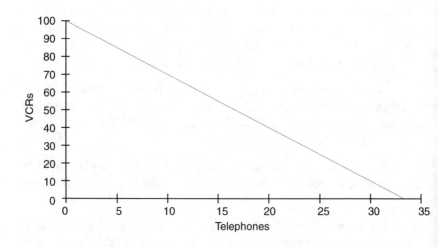

Figure 16.1 Japan's Production Possibilities Curve

If both countries try to be self-sufficient and neither trades, the production possibility curves are also their consumption possibilities curves.

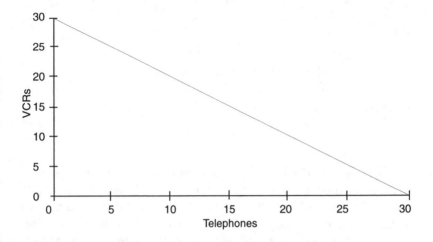

Figure 16.2 United States' Production Possibilities Curve

CONSUMPTION POSSIBILITIES CURVE
The curve shows all combinations of the two goods that the country can **consume**.

TRADING POSSIBILITIES CURVE
The trading possibilities curve shows all combinations of the two goods that the country could have if it specialized in the production of one good and traded for the other at the world exchange rate.

Assume now that trade opens up between Japan and the United States, and the world exchange ratio is 1 Telephone = 2 VCR. If Japan specialized in VCR production (producing 100), it could trade VCRs for as many as 50 telephones. This gives Japan's trading possibilities curve (see Table 16.5 and Figure 16.3). The U.S. could produce 30 phones if it specialized, but could trade for up to 60 VCRs (see Table 16.6 and Figure 16.4).

Japan's Trading Possibilities Curve

VCRs	100	90	80	70	60	50	40	30	20	10	0
Telephone	0	5	10	15	20	25	30	35	40	45	50

Table 16.5

United States' Trading Possibilities Curve

VCRs	60	54	48	42	36	30	24	18	12	6	0
Telephone	0	3	6	9	12	15	18	21	24	27	30

Table 16.6

The Interpretation of the Schedules–If Japan specialized in VCR production, it could produce 100 units. If it kept them all to itself, it would consume 100 VCRs, but no telephones. If it traded ten VCRs to the U.S., it would receive five telephones in return (at the exchange rate of 1T = 2VCR), allowing it to consume 90 VCRs and five telephones.

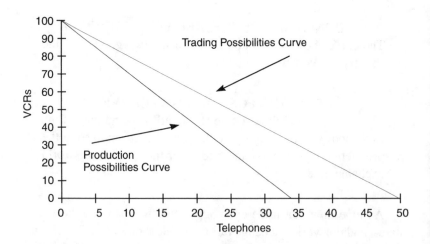

Figure 16.3 Japan's Production and Trading Possibilities Curve

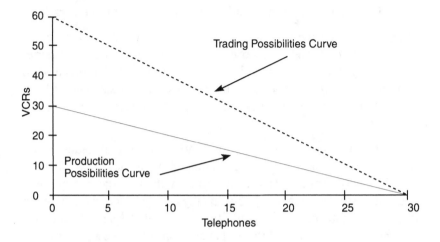

Figure 16.4 United States' Production and Trading Possibilities Curve

With specialization and trade, the trading possibilities becomes the new consumption possibilities curve.

Note the increased quantities of both goods that can be consumed, implying that each nation's overall standard of living will rise as a result of specialization and trade.

While some individuals may suffer from trade (telephone producers in Japan and VCR producers in the U.S.), the nation as a whole benefits (and the afflicted producers will be able to find jobs in the expanding sectors of their economies).

Tariffs, Quotas, and other restrictions on trade—A tariff is a tax applied to an imported good. Its effect is to raise the good's price. A quota is a limitation on the amount of a good that can be imported. Its effect is also to raise the good's price. Both tariffs and quotas make foreign goods less competitive with domestic products, hurting foreign producers while protecting domestic producers. The law of comparative advantage implies that any restrictions on trade will be harmful to a nation because it will limit the degree of specialization and hence the gains previously described.

Common Arguments made in favor of restriction on trade

Cheap Foreign Wages—It is frequently asserted that low foreign wages enable foreign industries to out-compete domestic industries. The inevitable result is that domestic producers will be forced out of business, American workers will lose jobs, and our standard of living will fall. Consequently, we need to provide protection for American industries.

The argument is almost wholly fallacious. The absolute level of wages is not what determines how competitive an industry is. Rather, it is the level of wages relative to the productivity of workers. If an American industry has high wages, but equally high productivity, it may very well be quite competitive with its foreign counterparts. In fact, it is high wage American industries that are some of our best performers in the international marketplace. The grain of truth in the argument is that some low wage foreign industries may, in fact, out-compete American industries, but this simply means that is where their comparative advantage lies and ours does not.

Infant Industry—The infant industry argument says that some new industries need time to develop the skills, techniques, and efficiency necessary to be "world-class." Failure to protect these industries will lead to their being "snuffed-out" before they had a fair chance. Protection of selected industries is alleged to be behind the rise to prominence of Japan, Taiwan, South Korea, and Singapore, and is a significant part of the case made for industrial policy. The argument is valid as far as it goes, but it does not explain how a country is able to separate the "winners" from the "losers." Some economists feel that what will happen in practice is that politically influential but senile industries will end up being protected.

Terms of Trade—There are certain conditions (whose description must await more advanced courses) where a country may benefit at the expense of others by using tariffs. However, these conditions do not always exist, and countries must be prepared for the imposition of retaliatory tariffs, which end up making everyone worse-off.

Antidumping—There is widespread belief that some foreign governments subsidize their industries to allow them to sell below cost (dump) in the United States. American industries are said to be victims of "unfair competition." What is seldom explained is why Americans should be upset if foreign governments help us buy products at low prices.

National Defense—The necessity of maintaining particular industries for national defense is often used as an argument to support protectionism. Like the infant industry argument, it is not illogical and cannot be completely evaluated in economic terms. Also like the infant industry argument, it suffers from the practical problem of how to identify those industries that are absolutely vital.

Problem Solving Examples:

Q Explain David Ricardo's Theory of Comparative Advantage. Give an example to illustrate the point of the theory.

A David Ricardo's Theory of Comparative Advantage states that the exchange (especially in international trade) is most efficient if each trader offers the particular good of which he has advantage in production relative to the good he receives in exchange. Alternatively stated, foreign trade is mutually beneficial, even when one nation is absolutely more efficient in the production of every good, as long as there are differences in the relative costs of producing the various goods in the two potential trading nations. Thus, the theory of comparative advantage is closely tied to the concept of opportunity costs.

As an example, assume that lawyer Smith can earn $35 an hour as a corporate lawyer. Assume further that he can type twice as fast as his secretary to whom he pays $6 an hour. But Mr. Smith can earn $35 an hour as a lawyer. Therefore, even if he has an absolute advantage in secretarial services, it is not worth his while to save $6 an hour in typing at the expense of $35 an hour as a lawyer. He would be better off using his training as a corporate lawyer, even if he is the most efficient typist in the office.

What is absolute advantage?

Absolute advantage exists when one nation can produce a good more cheaply and efficiently than another. Thus Brazil because of its climate, natural resources, and labor force has an absolute advantage over the United States in producing coffee while the United States has an absolute advantage over Brazil in producing computers.

16.3 International Finance

How International Payments are Made—Buying goods, services, or assets from foreign countries is complicated by the fact that countries use different currencies. Assume that an American consumer wants to buy something sold by the German producer. The German producer would be unwilling to accept American dollars in exchange for the product because American dollars are worth nothing in Germany. The company cannot pay its workers, supplies, or shareholders in that currency. In order for the exchange to take place, there must be some way to change dollars into German marks.

Banks play a crucial role as traders of currency. Americans can take dollars to the bank and exchange them for marks. Germans can take marks to the bank and exchange them for dollars. Since banks trade both ways, taking dollars for marks and marks for dollars, they are able to maintain reserves of both currencies, unless a persistent trade imbalance forces holdings of one currency down to zero. In the diagram (Figure 16.5), German consumers and American producers also rely on banks to provide the necessary currency trading services.

The buying and selling of foreign currencies is what is meant by the foreign exchange market. Its participants include banks and other financial intermediaries, consumers, business firms, and governments.

(Actually, international financial transactions can be a lot more complicated than the figure shows. For many years the dollar has held a special place in the world financial system as a "key" currency. This means that foreign countries have had such faith in the dollar that they have frequently conducted transactions in dollars rather than their own national currencies.)

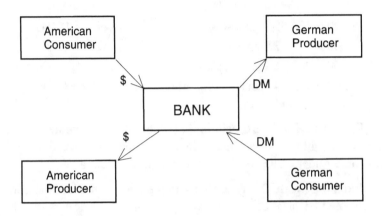

Figure 16.5 Making International Payments

Exchange Rate—The exchange rate is simply the price of one nation's currency in terms of another's. The table shows exchange rates existing between the U.S. dollar and selected other currencies on May 9, 1989. For example, $1 buys 2.158 Dutch gilders, therefore 1 gilder buys $.4639. A product costing $25.00 in the U.S. would cost 53.95 gilders; a product costing 100 gilders would cost $46.39. (This ignores transportation and transaction costs.)

Selected Exchange Rates

$1.00 = .6017 British pounds	1 pound = $1.662
$1.00 = 6.4615 French francs	1 franc = $.1548
$1.00 = 2.158 Dutch gilders	1 gilder = $.4639
$1.00 = 134.85 Japanese yen	1 yen = $.007416
$1.00 = 1.9153 German marks	1 mark = $.5221
$1.00 = 2433 Mexican pesos	1 peso = $.000409
$1.00 = 1.1864 Canadian dollars	1 dollar = $.8429

Exchange Rate Appreciation—If the dollar/gilder rate changes to $1 = 2.25 gilders, we say the dollar has appreciated. Each dollar will buy more gilders. The dollar has become more valuable.

Exchange Rate Depreciation—In the above situation, the gilder depreciated because each gilder will now buy fewer dollars than before.

Balance of Payments—The balance of payments is a summary statement of the transactions that take place between a country and the rest of the world during a given period of time.

The balance of payments uses a double-entry system of bookkeeping. Transactions are recorded as debits and credits. From the standpoint of the U.S., a debit transaction is one that requires us to supply dollars. Examples of debit transactions are:

1. Imports of goods and services.

2. Gifts made to foreigners (also known as unilateral transfers).

3. Acquisition of a long term asset or reduction of a long-term liability (e.g., stocks, bonds, real capital).

4. Acquisition of a short-term asset or reduction of a short-term liability (e.g., checking account balances or short-term bonds).

From the standpoint of the U.S., a credit transaction is one that causes foreigners to demand dollars. Examples of credit transactions are:

1. Exports of goods and services.

2. Gifts received from foreigners.

3. Sale of a long-term asset or long-term liability increased.

4. Sale of a short-term asset or short-term liability incurred.

All transactions are placed into specific categories. The simplest breakdown is between the current account and the capital account. The current account records all transactions involving goods and services. The capital account records all transactions involving short- and long-term assets. The balance of payment can be visualized as in Table 16.7.

	Debit	Credit
Current Account		
Capital Account		

Table 16.7 Schematic of the Balance of Payments Account

The beginning of wisdom regarding the balance of payments is to realize that **every transaction gives rise to both debit and credit entries**. Consequently, the balance of payments must always balance in an accounting sense. For example,

1. Americans buy $800,000 in automobiles from Germany, paying for them with dollar checks drawn on American banks. The import of goods leads to a $800,000 debit in the current account. The German acquisition of dollar demand deposits increases our short term liabilities and results in a credit of $800,000 to the capital account.

2. The French buy the equivalent of $2,000,000 in private American corporation bonds, paying for them with franc checks. The sale of the bonds (long-term assets) leads to a $2,000,000 credit in the capital account. The acquisition of francs (short-term assets) leads to a $2,000,000 debit in the capital account.

3. American tourists travel in Holland, spending the equivalent of $5,000 on souvenirs. The gilders spent were obtained by exchanging dollars at a Dutch bank. The souvenirs are an import resulting in a $5,000 debit in the current account. The Dutch have acquired dollars, leading to a $5,000 credit in the capital account.

If we sum all debits and credits, both sides will be equal.

Balance of Payments "Imbalances"—Balance of payments "imbalances" result from looking at just a portion of the ledger.

1. **Balance of Trade**—The net balance of debits and credits for goods.
2. **Balance on Current Account**—The net balance of debits and credits for goods and services.
3. **Balance on Capital Account**—The net balance of debits and credits for short and long term assets.

Exchange Rate Determination —Exchange rates are set in the foreign exchange market by the forces of demand and supply.

Demand Curve for Dollars—If the Dutch want to acquire our goods, services, and assets, they must acquire dollars. This is the basis of the demand curve for dollars. The more valuable the gilder, the greater the quantity demanded of dollars because a valuable gilder makes American goods, services, and assets a better buy to the Dutch.

Supply Curve of Dollars—If Americans want to acquire Dutch goods, services, and assets, they must acquire gilders. To do so, they must supply dollars. Here, the more valuable the dollar, the greater the quantity supplied. (More advanced treatments allow the supply curve to have a negative slope in some cases.)

Equilibrium—At the exchange rate of $1 = 2.25 gilders, the strength of the American dollar makes Dutch goods, services, and assets a good buy for Americans. The weakness of the gilder makes American goods, services, and assets less attractive to the Dutch. Consequently, there is an excess supply of dollars and that will drive down the exchange rate.

At the exchange rate $1 = 1.75 gilders, the weakness of the dollar makes Dutch goods, services, and assets a bad buy for Americans. The strength of the gilder makes American goods services and assets more attractive to the Dutch. Consequently, there is an excess demand for dollars and that will drive up the exchange rate.

At the exchange rate $1 = 2 gilders, quantity demanded equals quantity supplied and the market is in equilibrium.

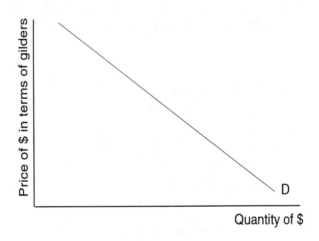

Figure 16.6 Demand Curve of Dollars

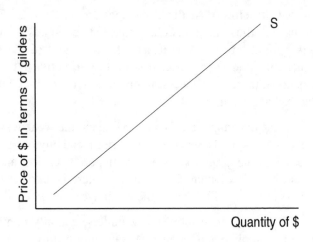

Figure 16.7 Supply Curve of Dollars

Shifts in the Curves—The foreign exchange market is unique in that frequently events can cause both curves to shift.

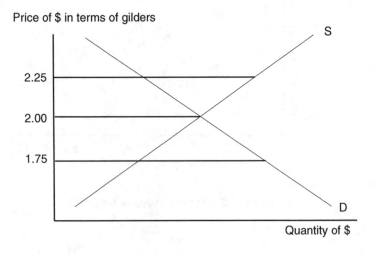

Figure 16.8 Equilibrium in the Market for Dollars

Factor	Event	Effect on D/S curve
Tastes	Dutch tastes for American goods increases	shift D curve out
	American tastes for Dutch goods increases	shift S curve out
Income	American income increases	shift S curve out
	Dutch income decreases	shift D curve in
Interest Rates	American rates increase	S shifts out D shifts out
Inflation	Higher inflation in U.S. than Holland	S shifts out D shifts in

Table 16.8

Purchasing Power Parity Doctrine—The purchasing power parity doctrine (PPP) says exchange rates will adjust to equalize the purchasing power of a unit of currency in all countries. For example, assume perfume sells for $20 a bottle in the U.S. and 50 gilders a bottle in Holland. PPP says the exchange rate will adjust to $1 = 2.5 gilders, so that both Americans and the Dutch are indifferent between buying the perfume in America or Holland. If the exchange rate was $1 = 3 gilders, perfume in Holland would cost Americans $16.67 and perfume in America would cost the Dutch 60 gilders. This would cause both countries to buy perfume in Holland and the gilder would appreciate in value. If the exchange rate was $1 = 2 gilders, perfume would be cheaper in America (can you calculate the price in gilders?). The demand for dollars would cause the dollar to appreciate. The only equilibrium is at PPP.

Exchange Rate Regimes—Exchange rate regimes refers to the system by which exchange rates are set.

Floating (Flexible) Exchange Rates—Under this system, exchange rates are solely determined by the market. The major advantage is that the market will automatically bring the flows of currency into equilibrium. If there is an excess supply of dollars (meaning foreign goods, services, and assets are relatively more attractive), the dollar will depreciate making these goods, services, and assets more expensive and reducing the quantity demanded.

Criticisms include:

1. Exchange rates become unpredictable, increasing the risk element involved in international trade.

2. Speculators will have too much influence on the market.

Fixed Exchange Rates—Under a fixed exchange rate system, every country sets the value of its currency in terms of every other one and pledges to take steps to maintain that exchange rate. For example, assume the U.S. dollar/British pound rate is set at ER1, but an increase in the demand for dollars (from D to D´) puts upward pressure on the rate. Either the U.S. or British government then must enter the market and supply enough dollars (Q2 – Q1) to keep the exchange rate at ER1.

The excess demand for dollars is frequently called the British balance of payments "deficit." This situation is a balance of payments "surplus" for the United States.

The major advantage of fixed exchange rates is that the future value of the exchange rate is known with certainty so that there is less risk associated with international trade.

The major disadvantage is that the exchange rate set may become "unrealistic," leading to persistent balance of payments, deficits, or surpluses. Deficits are the bigger problem.

In the example, if the British run persistent deficits at ER1:

a) If the British take responsibility for maintaining the exchange rate, they may eventually run out of dollars. Further, the dollars supplied may fuel inflation in the United States.

b) If the U.S. takes responsibility for maintaining the exchange rate, the dollars supplied may lead to domestic inflation.

Countries with persistent deficits may do several things:

1. Domestic economic policy may become "captive" to international concerns. A balance of payments deficit may force a country to raise domestic interest rates or reduce domestic income to decrease the demand for foreign goods, services, and assets.
2. There may be pressure for protectionism to stop the deficit.
3. The deficit country may be forced to "devalue" its currency. In the example, the British may give up on ER1 and begin supporting ER2. Devaluation may be the indicated policy in this case, but it is always a blow to national pride, and is contrary to what the system of fixed exchange rates is trying to accomplish.

"Dirty" Float—The current U.S. exchange rate system can be described as a "dirty" float. The exchange rate is allowed to be set by the market, but the government is prepared to intervene if the exchange rate gets "too far out of line."

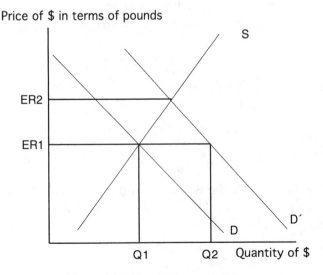

Figure 16.9 Fixed Exchange Rate

Gold Standard—Under the gold standard, gold is the internationally accepted currency and is used for trade. If one country's goods, services, and assets are deemed especially desirable by the rest of the world, gold will flow to that country. The influx of gold, because it adds to the country's money supply, will increase the country's price level and erode its favorable competitive position. The gold standard is equivalent to a system of fixed exchange rates.

Problem Solving Examples:

 What is the international balance of payments?

 The international balance of payments is an annual accounting statement, prepared by the various nations of the world. In it all the transactions which take place between a nation's residents (including individuals, businesses, and governmental units) and the residents of all other foreign nations are summarized.

Despite being called a "balance" of payments, this statement is more like a profit and loss statement than a balance sheet. On it a nation records all sales and purchases from foreign nations and accounts for any differences between sales (receipts) and purchases (expenditures).

Suppose an American firm sells a large piece of machinery to a British firm for $40,000. Describe the flow of money in this situation. Assume the exchange rate is $2 = £1.

Since the exchange rate is $2 for £1, the British importer must pay $40,000 \times \dfrac{£1}{$2} = £20,000$ to the American exporter.

To pay the £20,000, the British buyer draws a check on his demand deposit in a London bank for £20,000 and sends this to the American seller.

Since the American exporter cannot pay his/her expenses with pounds, he/she takes the check for £20,000 and sells it to some large American bank, probably located in New York, which is a dealer in foreign exchange. The American firm is then given $40,000 in demand deposits in the New York bank in exchange for the £20,000.

Finally, the New York bank deposits the check for £20,000 in a London bank for future sale.

Quiz: International Economics

1. A necessary assumption of the theory of comparative advantage if we are to prove gains from trade is

    (A) one country cannot have an absolute advantage in the production of both goods.

    (B) one country must be relatively more efficient in the production of one of the goods.

    (C) one country must be considerably larger than the other.

    (D) factors of production have to be free to move between countries.

2. Trade based on comparative advantage improves allocational efficiency because

    (A) less productive countries do not produce anything at all.

    (B) absolute efficiency determines which country will produce each product.

    (C) of specialization based on relative efficiency.

    (D) everyone and every country all benefit equally from it.

3. The infant-economy argument for tariff protection

    (A) is true if a country specializes in the production of only one good.

    (B) contradicts the theory of comparative advantage.

    (C) says that the long-run terms of trade are always shifting against agricultural products.

    (D) is valid if the production-possibility curve can be shifted outward in the direction of a new comparative advantage.

4. By the "terms of trade," we mean

    (A) the difference between exports and imports.

    (B) the ratio of exports to imports.

    (C) the difference between current account and capital account.

    (D) the ratio of export prices to import prices.

5. Which one of the following arguments for a tariff may be a valid economic argument, in the sense of benefiting all countries in the long run?

    (A) The peril-point tariff

    (B) The cheap-foreign-labor

    (C) The terms of trade

    (D) The infant industry

6.   An American tariff on linen will tend to

    (A)   raise U.S. real wages.

    (B)   help domestic linen producers and factors with a domestic comparative advantage in linen production.

    (C)   help nonlinen producers here.

    (D)   create deadweight loss to the degree that the consumer pays dollars to the tax collector.

7.   The purpose of governmental action to control foreign exchange and ration the inflowing foreign funds among producers might be to

    (A)   restrict imports and eliminate the balance of payments deficit.

    (B)   increase the value of domestic currency.

    (C)   develop the slow growing industries.

    (D)   All of the above.

8.   A serious problem with the Gold Standard system is that

    (A)   it poses a threat of severe inflation or depression as a result of the process of monetary adjustment.

    (B)   there is not enough gold in the world to make it a good medium of exchange.

    (C)   disequilibrium often persists.

    (D)   prices have a strong tendency to fluctuate.

9. The system of freely fluctuating exchange rates

    (A) is safer than the Gold Standard for those involved in international trade.

    (B) makes international trade a risky undertaking.

    (C) has a stabilizing effect on the economies.

    (D) improves a non-exporting nation's terms of trade.

10. Which of the following has a positive effect on the balance of payments?

    (A) Tariffs

    (B) Quotas

    (C) Reduction of imports

    (D) All of the above.

ANSWER KEY

1.	(B)	6.	(B)
2.	(C)	7.	(A)
3.	(D)	8.	(A)
4.	(D)	9.	(B)
5.	(D)	10.	(D)

The Best Test Preparation and Review!

GMAT CAT

6 Full-Length Practice Exams

Completely up-to-date based on GMAT CAT Exam Questions

Each written practice exam will provide a *score that is comparable to what you would achieve on the actual computer-adaptive test*

Prepares you for admission to MBA programs and graduate business schools

The *ONLY* test preparation book with answers explained in full detail to help you achieve a TOP SCORE

Comprehensive Reviews for Essay Writing, Math/ Quantitative, and Verbal Sections - plus drills

Expert test tips and strategies for taking Computer–Adaptive Tests

REA Research & Education Association

Available at your local bookstore or order directly from us by sending in coupon below.